मात्रालक्षणम्
MĀTRĀLAKṢAṆAM

कलामूलशास्त्र
ग्रन्थमाला
KALĀMŪLAŚĀSTRA
SERIES
(1)

General Editor
Kapila Vatsyayan

INDIRA GANDHI NATIONAL CENTRE FOR THE ARTS
NEW DELHI
and
MOTILAL BANARSIDASS PUBLISHERS PVT. LTD.
DELHI.

First Published 1988

Published by the Member Secretary for
INDIRA GANDHI NATIONAL CENTRE FOR THE ARTS
Central Vista, Janpath, New Delhi-110001

in association with

MOTILAL BANARSIDASS PUBLISHERS PVT. LTD.
Bungalow Road, Jawahar Nagar, Delhi-110007.

ISBN: 81–208–0585–2

Printed in India
at Shri Jainendra Press
A–45 Naraina Industrial Area Phase–I
New Delhi-110028

मात्रालक्षणम्

MĀTRĀLAKṢAṆAM

Text, Translation, Extracts from the Commentary, and Notes, Including References to Two Oral Traditions of South India

by

Wayne Howard

FOREWORD

Kalā Kośa Division of the Indira Gandhi National Centre for the Arts is the principal research and publication division. It will concentrate on the theoretical and textual tradition of intellectual discourse in the Indian artistic tradition. A distinctively Indian interdisciplinary system where the textual and the oral, the verbal and the visual, the scientific and the metaphysical, the transcendental and the functional were interlocked as parts of a whole is recognised, but its concepts, structure and processes are often difficult to identify. The Indira Gandhi National Centre for the Arts aims to comprehend the arts, within the context of the Indian world view, notions of space-time and interconnections at the level of theory and practice.

Emerging logically out of this perception are the four long range programmes of this division, namely, (i) *Kalātattvakośa* — A Lexicon of Fundamental Concepts and glossaries of technical terms; (ii) *Kalāmūlaśāstra* Series of fundamental texts basic to the Indian artistic traditions as also primary texts specific to particular arts; (iii) Publications, reprints, translations of works of critical scholarship such as those of A.K. Coomaraswamy; (iv) Encyclopaedia of the Arts — A multi-disciplinary, multi-volume Encyclopaedia of the Arts.

The Kalātattvakośa is the first of these programmes, complex, intricate in nature, but essential as a first prerequisite to identify fundamentals of a rare holistic system.

The Kalāmūlaśāstra is the second programme. Here critical editions of originals and translations of fundamental texts relating to the Indian Arts ranging from architecture, sculpture, painting, theatre, music, dance along with their scientific and technical commentaries will be undertaken. Attention in each of these volumes will be on the text unencumbered with the weight of some later obtuse commentaries and interpretations of a secondary nature. This series seeks to place the text in as exact a manner as is possible by considering all primary material available in any part of the world. In each case, microfilm and microfiche of the manuscripts have been obtained and made available to the editor for collation and editing. It is hoped that a new methodology of critically editing and collating texts will be established through the publication of the series.

Mātrālakṣaṇam is the first text to be published in this series. Perhaps it is one of the first attempts at transcribing the world's most complex system of orally accented verses which were transmitted through oral intonation into a written textual form. The transcribing of a complex code of oral intonation preserved through a most exacting recitative discipline presents challenges in arriving at an authentic text. The present volume is based on six damaged or incomplete manuscripts of the *Mātrālakṣaṇam* so far discovered, one printed edition in *Grantha* script (Krishnaswamy) and another in *Devanāgari* (B.R. Sharma). Obviously, the authenticity of a text cannot be restricted in this case to a mere collation of diverse recensions of a written text. It was necessary to recheck the written text with the few traditional *Sāmaveda* chanters. Indeed, as is known, the *Śruti,* i.e. the heard word has remained eternal and immutable in the Indian tradition while the written word has changed and is also subject to variations and inaccuracies. *Mātrālakṣaṇam* thus is a true indicator of the relationship of the syllable and the intonated word, of the articulated sound and the written word. For the contemporary scholar it is important to note that in the Indian tradition, the heard word was primary and the written secondary. Logically it leads to the deduction that the oral and the literate were not placed in a hierarchical framework of an evolutionary model of development from the oral to the literate. If so, then the broader classification of civilization being divided into pre-history and history on the basis of writing needs reassessment. *Mātrālakṣaṇam* importance is enhanced by the fact that it represents two very important *Śākhās* of *Sāmaveda,* namely, Rāṇāyanīya and Kauthuma *Śākhās.* As is well known, Patañjali mentions nearly one thousand *Śākhās* of the *Sāmaveda.* Of these, only three are now extant in the living oral tradition. Of these three, there is a close similarity between the Rāṇāyaṇīya and Kauthuma *Śākhās* in their mode of syllabic intonation as also their manuals for recitation.

The contents of the *Mātrālakṣaṇam* are of fundamental importance because this is perhaps the first text to discuss the concept of a time-unit measure *(mātrā).* The importance of *mātrā* as measure with the mathematical syllabic time value of vowels in their aspects of elongation, tempo, pitch and interval cannot be understood without taking into account sound as measure. In delineating the semantic relationship between syllable and letter, vowels and consonants, it lays the foundation of disciplines today recognised as phonetics, linguistics and prosody. Equally important is the discussion on sound and notes, in doing so it is a proto fore-runner of the 'modal' system of Indian music. As an exacting system of oral articulation and recitation, this text was used for recitation with hand gestures like *ārcika.* In relating the articulation of sound with body language, gesture, especially hands and fingers, the system of orally rendering a text according to its manuals, provides the basis of the emergence of a structure of artistic expression through the body (namely *āṅgikābhinaya*). In more senses than one, Vedic intonation is a precursor of both theory and practice (*śāstra* and *prayoga)* of the arts, in their original framework of interrelatedness.

Dr. Wayne Howard is an eminent scholar dedicated to Vedic studies and music. His earlier works have been acknowledged by western and Indian scholars. It was not an easy task to arrive at an authentic text from different recensions and oral intonations of different regions, but he has accomplished this difficult task. By providing staff notation he has facilitated comprehension by those trained in western techniques.

Despite its brevity, the preparation of the manuscript for publication, rechecking the text with traditional chanters, taking hard decisions of omitting of passages of the text on account of faulty language etc. has been a difficult matter. Apart from the traditional *Sāmavedic* chanters, other scholars like Dr. B.R. Sharma had to be consulted. Dr. C.R. Swaminathan, an eminent scholar in his own right, and his young colleagues have rendered inavaluable assistance. Thanks are acknowledged to Dr. C.R. Swaminathan and Dr. C.B. Pandey, Editor, IGNCA, for supervising the complex bilingual publication and Mr. K. Khosa for the jacket design.

New Delhi — Kapila Vatsyayan

10.11.88.

CONTENTS

PREFACE

As far as treatises on the Sāmaveda go, the Mātrālakṣaṇa ("Description of *Mātrā*") is considered a minor work; yet its importance in facilitating comprehension of the actual musical structure of the chants is unsurpassed. In it the principle of measurement by *mātrā* ("time unit") is put forth; extracts from the songbooks (*gānas*) serve to illustrate the various points. Chapter 1 deals first of all with the durations (short, long, or prolated/augmented) of syllables having a single notated numeral; it concludes with descriptions of syllables, each with two or more figures, that have a time value surpassing the two-*mātrā* limit that is a feature of the body of source verses (*ārcika*). Chapter 2 concerns itself by and large with exceptions to the rule that each number of these multi-figure syllables bears three *mātrās,* while Chapter 3 describes the conditions under which fractional durations are present. I have dealt with many of the treatise's statements in my *Sāmavedic Chant* (1977); however, I have since changed my opinion on the import of some passages. Hence the present translation does not merely repeat what has been written in the past.

To illustrate, as far as possible, the rules of the treatise, transcribed specimens of Kauthuma-Rāṇāyanīya chant from the Tanjore District in Tamilnadu and the North Kannara District in Karnataka are offered. The Tanjore style represented here is the strongest and most widespread sāmavedic tradition in all of India. The chanters employ a seven-tone scale with a central pitch located approximately in the middle of the gamut (pitches are relative); an eighth tone is heard but rarely.

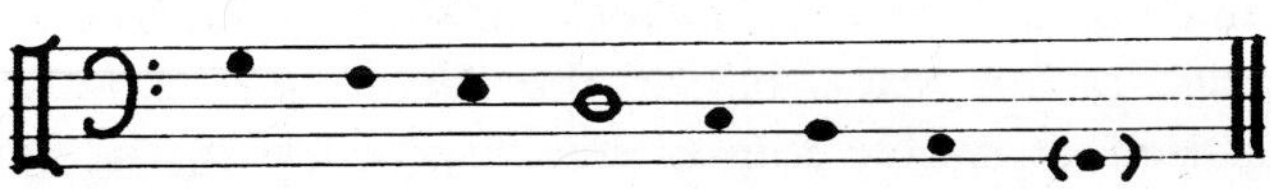

Adherents to this tradition call themselves Kauthumas, Gautamas, or Chāndosāmas; they may in fact be Rāṇāyanīyas, as are members of the Hāvik sect in North Kannara. These Sāmavedīs recognize a six-tone scale with intervallic relationships different from those of the Tanjore system, although a central pitch is prominent here as well.

Each music example in the notes to the translation shows which tradition is being illustrated, the type of note that is equivalent to one *mātrā*, the source and name of the chant from which the extract is taken, the notation, the metronomic indication, the pitch of the initial tone, and, in many cases, a formulation of overall divisions that may represent *mātrās* in a broader sense than that specified in the treatise. For example, the following fragment is from a transcription of the Rathantaram (Ūhyagāna 1.1.1), where a short syllable, under normal circumstances, is equivalent to an eighth note.

The notation 1r before 2 should last three *mātrās* (see the notes to Mātrālakṣaṇa 1.3); hence the syllable *śā* of this excerpt should theoretically have the duration of a dotted quarter note. However, it lasts instead the value of a whole note (eight *mātrās*). Nevertheless, three divisions, designated by the segmented beam above the syllable in question, are apparent. It is obvious, therefore, that in this and all performances of sāmavedic chant the value of the *mātrā* is not rigidly maintained (see the Translator's Postscript at the end of this book for a discussion of this relativistic view of timekeeping).

For the text and translation I have relied upon Oriental Institute (Baroda) Manuscript 11985, containing both text and commentary, and India Office (London) Burnell Manuscript 496k (Keith 4328), consisting of the text only. I have also benefited greatly from Prof. B. R. Sharma's edition of text and commentary.

The Baroda manuscript, the only manuscript source available with the commentary, was copied in the year 1447. In the *devanāgarī* script, it is a paper manuscript comprised of twelve folios. The disposition of the text on these twelve leaves is now presented. Decimal figures refer to chapter (*kaṇḍikā*) and precept (*śāstra*) of the Mātrālakṣaṇa, while C indicates texts of the commentary.

1r:	ōm / namaḥ sāmavedāya / athāto hrasvadīrghaplutamātrāny akṣarāṇi vyākhyāsyāmaḥ (1.1) . . . mātrāprakaraṇam vaktum iti kṛtvā āha / prasaṅgā° (1.1C)
1v:	°d yad uktam eva āha (1.1C) . . . dve mātre ardhaṃ cārdha° (1.5)
2r:	°tisras tisro mātrā ardhaṃ cārdhacatasraḥ (1.5) . . . ikārasya īkāraḥ (1.7C)
2v:	ukārasya ūkāra evaṃ (1.7C) . . . vṛttisamam ca gītaṃ sāmasu (1.14)
3r:	kartavyam (1.14C) . . . atisvāro maṃdraṃ pratyutkrāmati (1.19)
3v:	[pari]svāre vāsū3333 kay ā33 (1.19) . . . sunota (1.24C)

4r: so2mapāvnā3 o2333 (1.24C) . . . kruṣṭāt dvitīyam āgacchati ārohā°(1.31C)
4v: it[i] (?) rośabdaḥ prathamāt tṛtīyam āgacchati (1.31C) . . . prathamādir dvitīyādis tṛtīyādi° (2.1)
5r: °r iti prathamādir navamātraḥ (2.2) . . . na ghnatāvām ā gāyatre cāvanarde (2.5)
5v: ghnatā333vām ā33 abhi devām̐ iyā33333 (2.5C) . . . turaya11 to havaṃtā° (2.11C)
6r: °yi sahasradhāraṃ11 (2.11C) . . . nāy akramī33d vo3 agnā3yā33° (2.14)
6v: °yi tiyā33ñ cā3rā3333n (2.14) . . . varṇāntareṇoccāraṇāt / vyañjanavad ardha° (3.2C)
7r: mātrika ity evaṃ (3.2C) . . . ucce 'dhyardhāḥ / dīrghe hrasve (3.5)
7v: 'rddhaṃ yaṃ yaṃ (3.5) . . . manuṣye2° (3.6C)
8r: °bhir agniḥ ka īṃ vya2ktāḥ (3.6C) . . . janayaṃt sūryam api dīrgham (3.7C)
8v: abhigītakṛṣṭādir ardhamātrā nīcena svareṇa bhavaty (3.8) . . . atra vṛhāy o (3.9C)
9r: śakra iti vṛhā upadiṣṭā syāt (3.9C) . . . ākārī° (3.9C)
9v: °bhūte pratyaye nivṛttiḥ kathaṃ bhavati (3.9C) . . . tasmād uktam eva kārasyākāre (3.9C)
10r: nivṛttir iti (3.9C) . . . kathaṃ yaṃti gatiś cāṃtasthām āpadyata (3.9C)
10v: ity atra siddhavat (3.9C) . . . luptasya vyavastha (3.9C)
11r: ity anena bhogaḥ (3.9C) . . . saṃdher eva vikṛtaḥ (3.9C)
11v: śāstrāntare coktam (3.9C) . . . yasmiṃś cakita iṃdrādraḍā evam ā° (3.9C)
12r: °diṣu mātrārdhamātrikaṃ (3.9C) . . .

There are many mistakes in this manuscript, especially in the commentary portions; I have relied to a great extent on the corrections made by Prof. B. R. Sharma in his *devanāgarī* edition of both text and commentary (Sharma 1969).

The India Office manuscript, a paper document in the *grantha* script, is apparently a copy made by A. C. Burnell. It consists of two folios with the text only. The textual distribution is as follows.

1r: atha mātrālakṣaṇaṃ / athāto hrasvadīrghaplutamātrākṣarāṇi vyākhyāsyāmaḥ (1.1) . . . tṛtīyo dvitīyam atikramya prathamaṃ pratyutkrāmati punānāyām pu^{3}nā^{2}° (1.26)
1v: 31 caturvidho 'tikramo (1.26-27) . . . dvividhā (3.1)
2r: gatir igatir ugatiś ca (3.1) . . .

On occasion this copy omits some individual letters and syllables, but it is impossible to know if these mistakes are present in the original manuscript or if they resulted from the copying process. This source gives the notation of the chant quotations, although it has been necessary to consult Nārāyaṇasvāmī 1958 (and occasionally Dīkṣita 1967 for textual sources of some of the music examples) in order to obtain accurate readings. The Baroda text is devoid of the notation.

In the present work the notated specimens are given in the commentary or, if references are absent there, in the notes.

Finally, it is my pleasant duty to acknowledge the assistance of Prof. G. H. Tarlekar (Poona) and Prof. Lewis Rowell (Indiana University), both of whom spent a great deal of time reading the entire manuscript and offering many helpful suggestions and comments. I consider myself extremely fortunate to have had the benefit of their counsel. My sincere thanks go also to the India Office Library and the Oriental Institute at Baroda for furnishing microfilm copies of the manuscript described above.

ABBREVIATIONS

ĀrG	Āraṇyakagāna
ĀrGP	Āraṇyakagāna Pariśiṣṭa
GG	Grāmageyagāna
ML	Mātrālakṣaṇa
NK	North Kannara District, Karnataka
T	Tanjore District, Tamilnadu
ŪG	Ūhagāna
ŪhyG	Ūhyagāna (Rahasyagāna, Ūharahasyagāna)

INTRODUCTION

The Core Literature of the Sāmaveda

The essence of the Sāmaveda is chant (*sāman*); in the Mātrālakṣaṇa (ML) the various laws regarding duration refer specifically to these melodies, which appear in notated form in four chantbooks (*gānas*). The ML uses quotations from the chantbooks to illustrate its rules.

Most of the chants draw their texts from the *ārcika*, the collection of source verses (*ṛc*), which is divided into two parts. The first *ārcika* (Pūrvārcika) contains verses addressed to the gods Agni, Indra, and Soma Pavamāna, in that order. Each verse of the Pūrvārcika serves as the textual basis of one or more chants in the Grāmageyagāna (Village Chantbook). Attached to the end of this *ārcika* is the Āraṇyakasaṃhitā (Forest Collection), the verses of which are esoteric and philosophic in nature. The chants of the Āraṇyakagāna (Forest Chantbook) make use of consecutive verses of the Āraṇyakasaṃhitā, although chants based upon some Pūrvārcika texts are interspersed between. Intermingled with the chants on Pūrvārcika and Āraṇyakasaṃhitā texts are those consisting entirely of *stobhas*, extratextual matter that, to varying degrees, infiltrates many chants. The Āraṇyakagāna is divided into five sections (*parvans*: this term is used also for the "sections" of a chant) with the names *arka, dvandva, vrata,* and *śukriya.* A fifth section, a supplement or *pariśiṣṭa,* is added at the end.

The chants of the Grāmageyagāna and the Āraṇyakagāna are the basis (*prakṛti*) for the derivative (*vikṛti*) *sāmans* that occur in the other two chantbooks; hence the village and forest chants are sometimes called collectively the Prakṛtigāna. All of the melodies cited by the ML and its commentary are drawn from the Prakṛtigāna, although the present writer has utilized transcribed specimens from all four chantbooks for illustrative purposes.

The Ūhagāna (Chantbook of Modified [Melodies]) and the Ūhyagāna or Ūharahasyagāna (Chantbook of Modified Secret [Melodies]: known also simply as the Rahasyagāna) repeat melodies, albeit with occasional modifications, from the Grāmageya- and Āraṇyakagānas, respectively. The sectional division of the Ūha- and Ūhyagānas is according to the duration of the rituals for which their chants are intended. These divisions have the names *daśarātra, saṃvatsara, ekāha,* and *ahīna;* after them are the *prāyaścitta* and *kṣudra* sections, which present *sāmans* sung for expiation and for carrying out some particular wish, respectively.

The relationship of the four chantbooks to the two *ārcikas* is shown in the following outline.

I. Pūrvārcika + Āraṇyakasaṃhitā
  - A. Prakṛtigāna
    1. Grāmageyagāna (on Pūrvārcika texts only)

a. Āgneya-parvan
b. Aindra-Parvan
c. Pāvamāna-parvan

2. Āraṇyakagāna (on Pūrvārcika, Āraṇyakasaṃhitā, and *stobha* texts)
a. Arka-parvan
b. Dvandva-parvan
c. Vrata-parvan
d. Śukriya-parvan
e. Pariśiṣṭa

II. Uttarārcika

A. Uttaragāna (Vikṛti)

1. and 2. Ūhagāna (selected chants from the Grāmageyagāna) and Ūhyagāna (selected chants from the Āraṇyakagāna), each *gāna* divided into six sections:
a. Daśarātra-parvan
b. Saṃvatsara-parvan
c. Ekāha-parvan
d. Ahīna-parvan
e. Prāyaścitta-parvan
f. Kṣudra-parvan

As a rule, both of these posterior chantbooks repeat each melody three times, to different texts. The chant trilogy owes its existence to the requirements of the Vedic sacrifices, where the three statements of a *sāman* are sometimes repeated according to specified schemes. Moreover, in the sacrifices the five standard divisions (*bhaktis*) of each *sāman* are divided among three pre-selected Sāmavedic priests: the *prastāva* is sung by the Prastotṛ, the *udgītha* by Udgātṛ, the *pratihāra* by the Pratihartṛ the *upadrava* by the Udgātṛ, the *nidhana* by all three priests simultaneously. Two additional *bhaktis* result when the *hiṃkāra* (*him, hum,* or *hṃ)* is sung, by the three priests together, prior to the *prastāva* and when the sacred syllable *ōm* is intoned by the Udgātṛ before he sings the *udgītha.*

The most revered chant of the Sāmaveda, the Gāyatram, is somewhat of an anomaly in that it is the most recurrent chant of the two sacrificial *gānas* but yet does not appear in notated form a single time therein: the intricacies connected with the proper performance of this *sāman* (see Howard 1983: 321-25) were perhaps thought best kept secret from those who had not already undergone training as sacrificial functionaries.

As is the case with the other three Vedas (Ṛgveda, Yajurveda, Atharvaveda), the Sāmaveda can be taught only by members of the highest caste, Brāhmaṇa (Brāhmaṇ, Brāhmiṇ)—not to be confused with the *brāhmaṇa* class of literature. Sāmavedic Brāhmaṇs belong to the Kauthuma, Rāṇāyanīya, or Jaiminīya schools of singing: the ML is addressed to scholars of the Kauthuma and Rāṇāyanīya branches, the texts of which are closely related.

The Numeral Notation of the Kauthumas and Rāṇāyanīyas

The chantbook quotations in the ML make use of the numeral notation that is a feature of the Kauthuma-Rāṇāyanīya recension. The five basic figures (1–5) denote hand positions (*mudrās*) corresponding to the five fingers of the right hand: the thumb itself and the thumb touching the middle of the remaining fingers.

1 = the thumb, the first (*prathama* finger, held some distance above the forefinger.

2 = the forefinger, the second (*dvitīya*) finger,

3 = the middle finger, the third (*tṛtīya*) finger,

4 = the ring finger, the fourth (*caturtha*) finger,

5 = the little finger, the fifth (*pañcama*) or low (*mandra*) finger.

The sign 11, signifying not "eleven" but the figure 1 repeated, is called *kruṣṭa;* due to its infrequency, it is of secondary importance (for the *mudrās* associated with the symbol, see the notes on ML 1.28-31). Likewise, numeral 6, which denotes an "after-sound" *(atisvāra, atisvārya),* is not on a par with the five fundamental numbers. Figure 7 indicates 2 followed by 1 (*abhigīta*: See ML 3.4).

The thumb is "high" and the little finger "low" because of the sitting posture assumed by the chanter: he sits cross-legged with the hand resting, thumb on top, on the right knee. The numbers, then, signify hand postures, which invoke musical phrases and motifs *(svaras).* The reader is reminded that the Vedic *svara* is different from the *svara* of Indian classical music, where the term is used to denote scale degrees (*ṣaḍja, ṛṣabha, gāndhāra,* and so on). In the Sāmaveda a multitude of *svaras* belongs to each of the fundamental numbers *(mudrās);* hence the music that is heard in any given instance depends on the numerical context, the length of the vowel carrying the *svara,* and sometimes the *svara's* position within the chant section *(parvan).* It should be noted that the word *"mudrā"* does not appear a single time in either the ML or its commentary. But the *mudrā/svara* interconnection, which has been a characteristic of the chants from their inception and which has made possible the memorization and oral transmission of the *sāmans* down through the centuries, is so intimate and inseparable that distinguishing between the two was not thought necessary.

Occurring frequently in conjunction with the five basic numbers is the letter *r* (the zero, or *bindu,* is preferred instead in South Indian manuscripts), which designates syllables that are long (*dīrgha*: see ML 1.3 and the notes thereon)—as opposed to prolated (*pluta*) or augmented (*vṛddha*) syllables, that likewise have long vowels but that lack the *r*-notation. According to the Gujarātī Sāmavedīs now residing in Vārāṇasī, appearances of the letter *r* are accompanied by special left-hand *mudrās* (see Howard 1977: 81, Howard 1986: 218).

1r: The little finger of the left hand touches the palm as the thumb of the right hand is held some distance above the forefinger.

2r: The ring finger of the left hand touches the palm as the thumb of the right hand touches the middle finger.

3r: The middle finger of the left hand touches the palm as the thumb of the right hand touches the middle of the middle finger.

4r: The forefinger of the left hand touches the palm as the thumb of the right hand touçhes the middle of the ring finger.

5r: The thumb of the left hand touches the forefinger as the fingers close to form a fist; the hand is opened, then closed again. As this movement is executed, the thumb of the right hand touches the middle of the little finger. (Whether this opening and closing action of the left hand occurs with every appearance of 5r, or only in connection with the recurrent phrase

5r r
au ho vā,

I am unable to say at this time.)

The notational figures appear both above and within the text. This trait is apparent in the Grāmageyagāna's opening chant.

4 2r r 1 1 1 r2r
ognāi / ā yāhī3 voitoyā2i / toyā2i / gr̥ṇāno ha /
1 1 1 2r 1 1 3
vyadātoyā2i / toyā2i / nāi hotā sā23 / tsā2i bā234
5r r 3 5
au ho vā / hī234ṣī //

It is obvious here that some syllables have numbers placed above while others do not. ML 2.13 makes it clear that a number holds true for all subsequent syllables, until a different number appears. Thus, at the very beginning of the above *sāman,* numeral 4 (that is, the thumb of the right hand touching the middle of the ring finger) is valid for the syllables *o* and *gnāi.* It will be observed that a single line (*daṇḍa*) occurs after these syllables and also in seven other places in the course of the chant. These lines, which are vertical in the manuscripts, demarcate self-contained melodic entities and therefore divide the chant into sections (*parvans*): the above *sāman* is composed of nine *parvans,* but other chants may have more or less. A double *danda* marks the end of the chant. Within a given section a particular number (*mudrā*) may have influence on the musical realization of a neighbouring number. However, this influence does not extend from one section to another—the 4 on *gnāi,* for instance, has no effect whatsoever on the musical execution of the 2r on *ā,* at the beginning of the second *parvan,* and vice versa.

The numbers that are found within the text itself belong to the syllables that they immediately follow. Many syllables, therefore, are possessed of two or more figures, the number that is notated above and the number or numbers that ensue. In previous publications I have used the term "sequence" to apply to any combination of a superscribed number with one or more numbers in the text itself. Moreover, in writing about the sequences I have used, and shall continue to use, symbols like 3_{234} to specify particular combinations: in this case numeral 3 above a syllable is followed immediately by 2, 3, and 4 after the syllable (see *parvans* 8 and 9 in the above chant). In this case the thumb touches first the middle of the third finger, then the middle of the index, third, and ring fingers, in that order. Some sequences call for special *mudrās.* The pattern 2_3 (*praṇata*: see ML 3.3-5) of the second *parvan* in the afore-mentioned *sāman* signals the thumb moving from the base of the index finger to the tip of that finger (see Howard 1977: 80, 86). The sequence 1_2 (*karṣaṇa* or *preṅkha*: see ML 1.32) in the second, third, fifth, and sixth *parvans* calls for the thumb to glide over the middle joints of the remaining fingers, from the index finger to the little finger (see Howard 1977: 80, 85). The progression 1^2, sung the same as *karṣaṇa* or *preṅkha* in South India, elicits a special *mudrā* in the North: the thumb brushes against the index finger as the hand forms a fist (see Howard 1977: 80, 87). Another special finger movement is that connected with the three *svāra* sequences (1_{2345}^{111}, 2_{345}^{111}, and 3_{2345}^{111})—*svāra* not to be confused with *svara,* the designation for musical sound in general. *Svāra* (see ML 2.1-2) does not appear in the chant under discussion, but it occurs frequently in the Sāmaveda and indicates that the thumb is to pass over the tips of the remaining fingers (see Howard 1977: 80, 86).

The Source Verses

The Sāmavedic paṇdits not only chant the *sāman*s contained in the *gānas*; they also recite the original verses (*ṛcs*), which are present, as previously noted, in two "collections of *ṛc*" (*ārcikas*): the Pūrvārcika and the Uttarārcika. The Pūrvārcika is the textual source of the chants in the Grāmageyagāna and, along with the appended Āraṇyakasaṃhitā, the Āraṇyakagāna. The Uttarārcika, which repeats many verses from the Pūrvārcika, is the textual well from which the sacrificial chants of the Ūhagāna and the Ūhyagāna are drawn.

Practically all Sāmavedic chants show substantial modifications of the accented source verses on which they are based. For example, the original text of the chant previously under discussion is

1 1 !
agna ā yāhi vītaye gṛṇāno havyadātaye
1 !
ni hotā satsi barhiṣi //.

The principal accent, the *udātta,* does not have a special accent mark according to the accentuation method shown above, but it is normally preceded by the *anudātta* (marked by a horizontal line beneath a syllable) and followed by the *svarita* (shown by a vertical line above). The accentless syllables (*pracaya*) that often follow the *svarita* are, like *udātta* syllables, left undesignated.

The accentual scheme peculiar to Sāmavedīs of the Kauthuma and Rāṇāyanīya schools uses the figure 1 to designate the *udātta,* 3 to indicate *anudātta.* The *svarita* is specified by 2, but this number denotes *udātta* when an *anudātta* follows immediately. When two or more consecutive *udāttas* occur, only the first is marked with the 1, while 2r appears with the following *svarita*. *Pracaya* syllables have no markings whatsoever. The *ṛc* quoted above possesses the following figures according to this particular Sāmavedic system.

2 3 1 2 3 1 2 3 2 3 1 2
agna ā yāhi vītaye gṛṇāno havyadātaye /
1 2r 3 1 2
ni hotā satsi barhiṣi //

When this *ṛc* is compared to the above-cited chant, which is based upon it, the following textual differences are noticed.

1) *agna* (originally *agne*) becomes *ognāi*.
2) *ā yāhi* becomes *ā yāhī*.
3) *vītaye* becomes *voitoyāi / toyāi*.
4) *gṛṇāno* remains the same.
5) *havyadātaye* becomes *ha / vyadītoyāi / toyāi*.
6) *ni* becomes *nāi*.
7) *hotā* remains the same.
8) *satsi* becomes *sā / tsāi*.
9) *barhiṣi* becomes *bā au ho vā / hīṣī*.

The interjection *au ho vā* between the syllables of the last word is a *stobha*, an extra-textual addition to a Sāmavedic chant. Interpolations like this are quite common; as stated above, some chants are constituted entirely of *stobhas*. Among the other obvious changes that take place when a verse is converted into a chant are: (1) the replacement of vowels by other vowels, (2) the repetition of words or sections of words, (3) the distribution of a word over two or more *parvans*, and (4) the omission or addition of letters or syllables. These modifications were necessary in adapting the verses to the melodies—a fact which argues strongly for the pre-existence of the melodic fragments that constitute each and every chant.

ERRORS AND VARIANT READINGS

B = Oriental Institute (Baroda) Manuscript 11985
L = India Office Library (London) Burnell Manuscript 496k (Keith 4328)
S = B.R. Sharma, ed. *Mātrālakṣaṇa, with Commentary.* Tirupati: Kendriya Sanskrit Vidyapeetha, 1969.

Note: The letter C following the decimal references refers to the ML commentary.

1.1 L: hrasvadīrghaplutamātrākṣarāṇi
1.3 L: hrasvamātrā
1.4 L: dīrghan tu mātrāsaṃyogād
1.4C B: sāmarājana
1.5 L: mātrādhañ cārdhacatasraḥ
B: praṇavo
1.6 L: ity te
B: catvāraḥ svarāḥ
1.6C B: eva iti
S: eta eva catvāro for the B reading eta iti catvāro
S: aniyamāt for the B reading aniyamatvāt
B: ata eva ity uktam
1.8 B: saṃdhyakṣarāṇi āha
1.8C B: ākārāt abhiniṣpattiḥ
S: sūktā for the B reading sūktāni sunāminī
1.11C S: drutādayaḥ for the B reading drutā
1.15C S: uccāraṇāsāmarthyāt kevalaḥ for the B reading uccāraṇasāmarthyāt kevalasya
1.16C S: svare svare
1.17 B: pratyutkramātikramakarṣaṇaḥ svāreṣu
1.19 B: svāre instead of parisvāre
L: v$\overset{2}{\bar{a}}$343 (an incorrect notation)
B: vā3333 kay ā33[?]sthā33[?]yirā3333n
1.19C B: mantram instead of mandram
B: viṣayo
S: siddhaḥ śāstrāntare for the B reading siddhi-śāstrāntare
1.20C S: sudāvo ity etāni for the B reading pradhāprajātāni
1.21C S: adds the bracketed portion
1.28 B: ū33 na ā3 gā3[?]333hī3
1.29 B: āro33hām̐
1.30 B: yajñā33ya
1.31 B: ī33 hī3 hī3 hī hī hi
1.31C B: kruṣṭādi dvitīyam

S: antarāyati for the B reading taṃtāiyati

S: pramāṇopajñātāni for the B reading pramāṇoprajñātāni

1.32 B: bo3dhā33 / ā333yiṃdrā3 / nmā3333bhā3[yi] / o3333[3]yi / tvaṃ tvā33m e /

L: b$\overset{1}{\text{o}}$dhā23 (an incorrect notation)

2.2 B: harī33[?]śrī33111 / rayā33[?]111yim / ī23111 /

2.5C S: pratiprasavaḥ for the B reading prati sataḥ

2.6C S: saṃdhivat for the B reading satyaṃ naṃ

2.7C S: u vām iti for the B reading mrjaṃti

2.9C S: adds bhavataḥ

2.10C B: svarau for svāre

2.13 B: gṛṇā3[?]no2 ha / draviṇasyur vipanyayā2[2] / vipāṃ jyo2tā3yi / ā2d it pratnā33[?]sya retasāḥ / agniṃ vo vṛdhā3ntā3m /

2.13C S: adds pañcasvaraiḥ (bracketed)

2.14 B: o3gnā3yi / preṣṭhaṃ vo hā3u / ṣu prā3vo333cā3333ḥ / nāy akramī33t / vo3 agnā3yā33yi / tiyā33[?]ñ cā3[?]rā3333n / viśo viśo hum vo33 atithā33[?]yim /

3.1 B: dvividhā gatir bhavati / [igatir] ugatiś ca

3.1C B: kaṃṭhyā ā i u iti kāṃṭhyoṣṭhyā / ā iti kāṃṭh[y]a-tālavyā

3.2 B: trimātrikaś ca ī[?]mātrikaś

3.2C S: āgatānām for the B reading āmānāṁ

S: manyate for the B reading mante

3.3C S: dīrghavat kuryād ity uktam for the B reading vaktuyād ity uktam

3.5 L: vinatapraṇatayor ante

B: yaṃ yaṃ yāṃ ya3ṃ

3.6 L: mandre ['dhyardhā]

3.6C B: ṛksvaravid

3.7 B: prathame dvitīye 'dhyardhā

3.8 L: abhigīte kruṣṭādir

B: abhigīte kṛṣṭādir

3.9 L: 'ṇumātrā rādhāyāṃ

3.9C S: sahāṇumātra uktaḥ for the B reading sahāṇumātrr uktaḥ

S: svaro 'ntar bhūtaḥ for the B reading svarāntar bhūtaḥ

S: mātṛkāparimāṇāt for the B reading mātṛkāt parimāṇāt

S: svaravarṇanaṃ parikaroti for the B reading svāvarṇanāparikarodi

मात्रालक्षणम्
Mātrālakṣaṇam

मात्रालक्षणम्

विवरणसमन्वितम्

प्रथमा खण्डिका

अथातो ह्रस्वदीर्घप्लुतमात्राण्यक्षराणि व्याख्यास्यामः ।।१।।

मात्राक्षराणि

मात्रालक्षणं नामेदं शास्त्रं परिशिष्टम्। शास्त्रस्य परिशिष्यमाणमर्थं वदतीति परिशेषः। कस्यार्थः परिशिष्यते? मात्रालक्षणं वाच्यमिति। कुतः एतत्? स्मृतितः प्रतीयते —

पदं पादं विधां मात्रां छन्दो विज्ञाय दैवतम्।
आर्षं च ब्राह्मणं चैव ततः साम प्रयोजयेत्।।
अक्षरज्ञो विरामज्ञः प्रत्यारम्भी तथैव च।
स्वरमात्राविभागज्ञः स विप्रो गानमर्हति।।

ततः तथा (अथ) इदानीं तदुच्यते। यद्येवं मात्रा च-[अक्षर]-कालो भवतीत्येवं प्रकृतौ कृत्वा न वक्तव्यम्।

अथातः कार

उच्यते — न तत्र मात्रालक्षणमुक्तम्। किं तर्हि? तत्र संज्ञाप्रकरणं प्रकृतम्। तेन प्रसङ्गेन ह्रस्वादीनां प्रस्तावः। अक्षराणां ह्रस्वदीर्घप्लुतानां सा चेष्यते बहुप्रकार [त्वाद] क्षरस्य। तस्मात् प्रसङ्गान्मात्राधिकारार्थं तदुक्तम्।

बहुप्रकारस्य

मात्राप्रकरणं वक्तुमिति कृत्वा आह। प्रसङ्गाद्यदुक्तम् [तद्] एव आह। न कृत्स्नम्। उक्तं यत् ''मन्द्रद्वितीयतृतीयैः स्वरैः'' इति तद् द्विमात्रा द्विर्विनतप्रणतोत्स्वरिताभिगीतानां च विशेषतोक्तम्। तथा स्वारे त्रयोऽन्त्याः।

विशेषोक्त

पृथगंकमात्रा इति। तस्मादेवमादीनि परिशिष्यन्ते इह अनुक्तानि। तत इदमारभ्यते — 'ह्रस्वदीर्घप्लुतमात्राणि'। मात्राशब्दः परिमाणवाची। ह्रस्वदीर्घप्लुतपरिमाणानि अक्षराणि व्याख्यास्यामः कथयिष्याम इत्यर्थः ।।१।।

सामस्वर्धमात्रमणुमात्रं च।।२।।

सामसु सामविषये अर्धमात्राकं कालमामनन्ति। अणुमात्राकं [च]। तद् व्याख्यास्यामः ।।२।।

अणुमात्रिकं

ह्रस्वं मात्रा। दीर्घं द्वे। प्लुतं वृद्धं चेति त्रिमात्रमभिधीयते।।३।।

ह्रस्वं द्विमात्रसंयुक्तं प्लुतमाहुर्मनीषिणः।
दीर्घं तु मात्रासंयोगाद्वृद्धमित्यभिधीयते।।४।।

CHAPTER 1

1. Now henceforth we shall explain the syllabic sounds having the durations short, long, [and] prolated.

Commentary:

The Mātrālakṣaṇa is a supplementary treatise. "That which has the purpose of reporting supplementary teaching" is a supplement. For what [specific] reason is a supplementary work [necessary]? "The Mātrālakṣaṇa is to be addressed [in this regard]." Why [was] this [treatise written]? [That which] follows [should be] called to mind.

> One should employ the *sāman* after knowing the word, the quarter-verse, the division, the time-measure, the meter, the deity, the sage connected with it, and the Brāhmaṇa [text].
>
> That Brāhmaṇ is fit to chant [*sāmans*] who knows the syllables, the pause, the recommencement, and also the sound, the time-measure, and the partitions.

Therefore now that which is addressed [by the Mātrālakṣaṇa]. This is assuredly time measurement and letter duration; thus elaborating on the *prakṛti* [(that is, the Grāmageyagāna and the Āraṇyakagāna)] is not to be discussed. [The formation of the Prakṛtigāna] is [already] spoken of [in other treatises on the Sāmaveda]. [It] is not discussed in the Mātrālakṣaṇa. What, then, [does the treatise address]? In it clear explanation is provided. The introductory [rules are concerned] with the incidence of short [syllables], and so on; and the [duration] of short, long, and prolated syllables is given. From the occurrence of many types of syllables the rationale of temporal relationships is discussed. Endeavouring "to relate explanation of time measure" used to be spoken about. By means of the [typical] case, what is discussed [in the treatise] is precisely that which used to be expressed [in learned discourse]. The entire [Prakṛtigāna] is not [discussed] . . . . "We shall relate [the explanation of topics concerning duration]" is the [stated] goal [of the treatise].

2. In the Sāmavedic chants the one-half and one-quarter durations are found.

Commentary:

With regard to the *sāman* chant, [the chanters] are cognizant of a time value consisting of one-half *mātrā* and [also one of] one-quarter *mātrā*. This we shall explain.

3. A short [syllable is worth] one *mātrā*. A long [syllable is worth] two [*mātrās*.] [A syllable having] triple measure is called "prolated" or "augmented."

4. The wise men used to say [that] a short syllable with two *mātrās*

तत्र प्लुतवृद्धयोर्द्वयोरपि [अभेद] ग्रहणादभेदयमाशङ्क्य विनिवृत्त्यर्थम्। मा भू [त्] संज्ञाभेदात् कालभेद इति। स प्लुतः प्रान्त्ययोः राज [योः] प्लवत प्लवते — ''आता ऽ ३ प्ताता'' इत्येवमादिषु ।।३-४।।

सामराजनि

मात्रार्धमात्रा चाध्यर्धा नाम।

द्वे मात्रे अर्धं चार्धतिस्रः। तिस्रो मात्रा अर्धं चार्धचतस्रः।

प्रणवेऽर्धचतस्रो मात्राः।

मात्रायाश्चतुर्थोंऽशोऽणुमात्रा नाम।।५।।

चतुर्थांशाणु

सामतः प्रत्येतव्या। ''ह्रस्वदीर्घप्लुतमात्राण्यक्षराणि व्याख्यास्यामः'' (मा॰ल॰ १.१)। तत्र प्लुतवृद्धयोः त्रिमात्राकः काल उक्तः। ''प्लुतं वृद्धं चेति त्रिमात्रमभिधीयते'' (मा॰ल॰ १.३) इति। क्व पुनरर्द्धचतस्रो मात्रा

त्रिमात्रिकः

भवन्ति? [प्रणवे]। 'अणुमात्रा' इति इयं संज्ञा ।।५।।

इयंसंज्ञाणुमात्रेति

अइउऋ इत्येते ह्रस्वाश्चत्वारः।।६।।

अऋइउ

एत इति परिसंख्यानार्थम्। एत एव चत्वारो नान्य इति। कुतो नान्येषां प्राप्तिरिति। कालसामान्यात् मात्रा (णाम्)।

मात्राणि

अत्र केचिद्विनिवेशं मन्यन्ते। तेषां त्वनियमत्वात्। पुनरनुप्रदानव्यञ्जनानां तेषामर्द्धमात्रिकः कालः। अन्येषां मात्रिक

अनियमात्

इति। मा भूत्तेन व्यञ्जनानामिति। ह्रस्वसंज्ञा कालतुल्यतः। अतः एत इत्युक्तम् ।।६।।

एत एव सवर्णे प्रत्यये दीर्घा भवन्ति।।७।।

अत्र (एते) एव अकारादयः सवर्णे प्रत्यये दीर्घा भवन्ति। [अकारस्य] अवर्ण एव सवर्णः। तथा परेषामपि। ऋकारस्य ॠकारः। इकारस्य ईकारः। उकारस्य ऊकारः। एवम्।।७।।

अत एव संध्यक्षराणि।।८।।

संध्यक्षराण्यभिनिष्पद्यन्ते। तानि च दीर्घाणि भवन्ति। [अतः] अकारादभिनिष्पत्तिः। सूक्तं ''सुनामिनी

added is a prolated [syllable]. But a long [syllable] is called "augmented" due to the addition of one *mātrā* [to this syllable].

Commentary:

. . ."Two different ways of measuring time" [and not "two different time values" is to be inferred from the distinction between "prolated" and "augmented"]. In the Sāmarāja [-*sāmans*] there is prolation in the two endings. Similarly in other such cases also [it is seen].

5. One *mātrā* plus one-half *mātrā* is called *adhyardha;* two *mātrās* plus one-half [*mātrā* is called] *ardhatisra;* three *mātrās* plus one-half [*mātrā*] is called *ardhacatasra;* three and one-half *mātrās* [occur] on the *praṇava* [(i.e., on the sacred syllable *ōm)*]; the one-quarter portion of a *mātrā* is called *aṇumātrā.*

Commentary:

[These time values] are to be understood as referring to the *sāman* chant. "We shall explain the syllabic sounds having the durations short, long, [and] prolated." There the three-*mātrā* time value of prolated and augmented [syllables] is stated. "[A syllable having] triple measure is called 'prolated' or 'augmented.'" But where are three and one-half *mātrās* found? On the *praṇava.* "*Aṇumātrā*" is that appellation [that refers to the quarter portion of a *mātrā*].

6. *A, I, U, Ṛ* : These short [vowels] are four [in number].

Commentary:

"These" [is used] for the sake of enumeration. "Exactly these four and no others [are short]." "But wherefore is the validity of the other [vowels]?" From the rest time measure and melody [arise]. In this regard some consider the putting down of [these] durations [in a book]. Then [there are durations] which arise due to irregularity. Of them, moreover, is the one-half *mātrā* value of emitted consonants. One time unit [is characteristic] of the rest. Let [this short time value] not be [confused] with that of the consonants. The appellation "short" is due to the similarity of time. Hence "these" [*(ete)*] is addressed.

7. Those very [vowels] subsequent [to the short vowels, and] in the same [respective] phonetic classes, are long.

Commentary:

In this regard [those] very vowels subsequent to [the short vowels] *a,* and so on, [and] in the same [respective] phonetic classes, are long. The vowels *a* and *ā* alone belong to the same phonetic class. In like manner the succeeding [long vowels] are obtained: *ṝ* [follows] *ṛ, ī* [follows] *i, ū* [follows] *u.* Thus.

8. Hence the diphthongs also [are long].

संध्यम्'' इति। सूक्तं सुष्ठूक्तम्।

स्वरस्य वैस्वर्यं न व्यञ्जनस्य ।।९।।

स्वरस्य अकारादेः नानास्वरा भवन्ति। न व्यञ्जनस्य ।।९।।

स्वरश्च स्वर्यते ।।१०।।

आर्चिके च स्वर एव स्वर्यते न व्यञ्जनम्। अथवा स्वरस्य एतदभिधानम्। स्वराणां स्वरितं यस्मात्तस्मात्स्वर
स्वरिते
इत्युच्यते ।।१०।।

तिस्रो वृत्तयो भवन्ति। द्रुता मध्यमा विलम्बितेति। द्रुतायां वृत्तौ त्रिकला मात्रा भवति। चतुष्कला मध्यमायाम्। पञ्चकला विलम्बितायाम्। द्रुता रोहिणी। श्यामा मध्यमा। श्वेता विलम्बिता ।।११।।

विशेषार्थं प्रक्रियन्ते द्रुता रोहिणी। मध्यमा श्यामा। विलम्बिता श्वेता। वर्णा उच्यन्ते रोहिण्यादयः ।।११।।

तासां देवताः। वायव्या द्रुता वृत्तिः।
बार्हस्पत्या मध्यमा। सौरी विलम्बिता ।।१२।।
तासु मात्राकालस्तिसृष्वेकः ।।१३।।

तासु वृत्तिषु मात्राकालस्तिसृष्वेकः। (एक) एव कालो भवति ह्रस्वदीर्घवृद्धानाम् ।।१३।।

वृत्तिसमं च गीतं सामसु ।।१४।।

कर्त्तव्यम् ।।१४।।

दीर्घे वृद्धे चोपधौ गत्याः पृथक्कालः ।।१५।।
उपध्यै

Commentary:

From the vowel *a* the diphthongs appear. They also are long. The existence [of the diphthong] is due to the [prefixed] *a*-vowel. [When] properly uttered it has the apropriate name *"sandhyam"* [(i.e, based on *sandhi,* "euphonic combination," because of its joining of two simple vowels)].

9. [There are] various sounds of the vowels [but] not of the consonant.

Commentary:

Of the vowel *a,* and so on, there are different sounds, [but] not of the consonant.

10. Just the vowel is sounded.

Commentary:

So in the *ārcika* only the vowel is sounded, not the consonant. Or one might say that this is why *svara* [("vowel"="sound")] has its name. "Sound [is obtained] from any of the vowels having the sounded [accent]," it is said.

11. There are three tempi: fast, moderate, slow. In the fast tempo a *mātrā* has three *kalās,* in the moderate four *kalās,* in the slow five *kalās.* The fast [tempo] is red, the moderate dark blue, the slow white.

Commentary:

On account of the difference [of the tempi, they] are performed fast, etc. The colours [associated with the tempi] are said to be red, etc.

12. They are related to the gods. The fast tempo belongs to Vāyu, the moderate to Bṛhaspati, the slow to Sūrya.

13. Among these three [tempi], there is one [and only one] time value of the *mātrā* [in any given tempo].

Commentary:

Of short, long, and augmented [syllables], the duration of a *mātrā* is the time value [associated with] only one among the three tempi.

14. In the *sāman* chants there is melody and evenness of tempo.

Commentary:

[This is] the obligation [of the chanter].

15. There is separate time measurement of *gati* on [its] addition to long and augmented [syllables].

तत्र गतेः पराधीनत्वाद्वर्णान्तरेणोच्चार्यते। उच्चारण(।)सामर्थ्यात् केवलस्य। तत्र दीर्घे (ण) वा उच्चार्यते। वृद्धेन वा। ''औ होयित्वामिद्धि हवामहा ^३ ए'' (आ.गा. २७)। तथा ''आयिपुना ३'' (ग्रा.गा.
वृद्ध
१४.५.५११.५) एवमादिषु। दीर्घे वृद्धे वा उपधो [च्चारणे] गत्याः पृथक्कालो भवति। अनुच्यमाने ऽप्येवमेव भविष्यति। वर्णपृथक्त्वात्। आह। यदि वोच्यते। तथा सति व्यञ्जनधर्मित्वात् गतिर्नैव स्यात्। भूयांसश्च व्यञ्जनस्वराः। अधिकत्रिमात्रो नानास्वरीभूतो व्यञ्जनसहितः एक एवाक्षरं भवति। युक्तत्वात्। न पृथक् कालः स्यात्। अतः पृथक्काल इत्युक्तम् ।।१५।।

विस्वरमक्षरं स्वरे स्वरे त्रिमात्रं भवति ।।१६।।

नानास्वरैः संयुक्तमक्षरं क्रुष्टादिषु स्वरे [षु] त्रिमात्रं भवति ।।१६।।
क्व पुनर्नानास्वरे संयोगोऽक्षरस्य ? [अत] आह —

प्रत्युत्क्रम-अतिक्रम-कर्षणाः-स्वारेषु ।।१७।।

क्राम

प्रत्युत्क्रमोऽष्टविधः ।।१८।।

तत्र प्रत्युत्क्रमोऽष्टप्रकारो भवति ।।१८।।

५ ३ २ ^ ४
अतिस्वारो मन्द्रं प्रत्युत्क्रामति परिस्वारे। ''वा ६५६ कया३स्थाऽ५यिरा ६५६
परिस्वारं
न्'' ।।१९।। (ग्रा.गा. १.२.१३.१) ।।१९।।

मन्द्रं प्रत्युत्क्रामति परिस्वारे विषये। परिस्वारः सिद्धः शास्त्रान्तरे ''मन्द्रोहिनुहिभूतस्तु परिस्वार इति स्मृतः''। इति
परिस्वार सिद्धिः
नारदीयशिक्षायाम्। अत्र हि इति उत्कृष्टार्थः। प्रत्युत्क्रमात्। वायुः जावानो हो३। ''मतौऽ२१ हुवाइ। औऽ३होऽ२३४वाऽ६५६''। वायोराऽ२३नी। कयाऽ३स्थाऽ५इ राऽ६५६ न्''। ''वायोरनीके अस्थिरन्'' ।।१९।।

Commentary:

There, on account of *gati*'s dependence upon [a preceding long or augmented syllable, it] is pronounced by means of a letter change. Due to the fitness of pronunciation merely of itself, it is uttered either with long or with augmented [syllables]. [An example of its attachment to a long vowel is found in the extract]

2r r r r 2
au hoyi tvām id dhi havāmahā3 e [ĀṛG 14.1: Bṛhat Sāma)].

Likewise, [an example of its attachment to an augmented syllable is found in the excerpt]

4 5 4
āyi punā [(GG 511.5: Aiḍam Āyāsyam),

and] thus elsewhere. There is separate time measurement upon the added pronunciation of *gati* to a long or an augmented [syllable]. On not being uttered [with the vowel that immediately precedes, *gati*] certainly will be like this. In other words, [that which] is uttered [the chanter] says by [speaking] the individual letters one by one. Likewise, a final consonant should not be [considered a part] of *gati*. The consonant and vowels [of a syllable with *gati*] are increased [due to the addition of a final consonant]. The occurrence of two different vowels totalling three *mātrās*, joined to a [preceding] consonant, is [considered] only one syllable. From [pronunciational] employment [they are thought of as one syllable]. [They are] not separate [syllables]. Hence "separate time measurement" is addressed.

16. A syllable divorced from accentuation has triple measure on every *svara*.

Commentary:

A syllable connected with different *svaras—kruṣṭa,* and so on—has triple measure on every *svara.*

17. [The various *svara* combinations are found] in *pratyutkrama*, *atikrama*, *karṣaṇa*, and *svāra*.

18. There are eight types of *pratyutkrama*.

19. In the [number combination] *parisvāra*, the *atisvārya* [*mudrā*] ascends to the low [*mudrā*]. [Instances of *parisvāra* include] *vā* [and] *kāy āsthāirān*.

Commentary:

Within the compass of *parisvāra,* ascent is made to the low [*mudrā*]. [Having] established [the meaning of] *parisvāra,* [the author], at the end of the precept, gives examples of ascent to the low [*mudrā*]. *Pratyutkramas* [involving such ascent] include [passages on the excerpts] *vāyuḥ javāno ho* [and] *vāyor anīke asthiran.*

मन्द्रश्चतुर्थम् ''श्रायन्तस्तरोभिः पुरः'' ।।२०।।

५ २ ५ ५ २ २ ५
''श्रायन्त इव सू ४ रायाम्'' (ग्रा.गा. ७.४.२६७.१)। ''तरोभिर्वो विदा४द्वासूम्'' (ग्रा.गा. ६.१.२३७.४)।
५ २ २ ५
''पुरोजिती वो४ऽधासाः'' (ग्रा.गा. १६.८.५४५.६)। सू-दा-वो इत्येतानि उदाहरणानि।।२०।।
'प्रधाप्रजातानि' उदाहरणानि)

चतुर्थस्तृतीयं ''दूतं देवो माना'' ।।२१।।

५ २ ४ ५ २ ४ ५ २ ४
''दूता ३०'' (ग्रा.गा. १.२.१२.१) ''देवो ३'' (ग्रा.गा २.६.५५.१)। ''माना ३'' (ग्रा.गा ३.२.१२८.२)।
ता-वो-ना इत्येतान्यक्षराणि [उदाहरणानि] अत्र चतुर्थस्वारास्तृतीयं प्रत्युत्क्रामन्ति ।।२१।।

तृतीयो द्वितीयं ''हीष्यादौ'' ।।२२।।

३ ५
''हीऽ२३४षी'' (ग्रा.गा. १.१.१.१)। अत्र हीशब्दस्तृतीयो द्वितीयं प्रत्युत्क्रामति ।।२२।।

द्वितीयः प्रथमम् ''औहो अग्न'' इति ।।२३।।

२ २ २ १ १
''औ हो १इ अग्ने राथाऽ२३म्'' (ग्रा.गा. १.१.५.२) इत्यत्र हो शब्दः द्वितीयस्वरात् प्रथमं प्रत्युत्क्रामति ।।२३।।

मन्द्रश्चतुर्थमतिक्रम्य तृतीयं प्रत्युत्क्रामति संधौ सुनोतसोम पा०ने ।।२४।।

४ ३२ ४ ५ २ २ ३ २ २ ३ ५
संधौ संधिविषये ''सुनोत सोमपा। आ०ना ओ २३४ वा'' (ग्रा.गा. ८.६.२८५.२) इति। [अत्र] पा-शब्दः मन्द्रा [त्] तृतीयं प्रत्युत्क्रामति ।।२४।।

20. The low [*mudrā* ascends] to the fourth [*mudrā*, as in the excerpts] *śrāyantas, tarobhiḥ,* [and] *puraḥ*.

Commentary:

[Examples of *pratyutkrama* from 5 to 4 include]

5r 5
śrāyanta iva sū4rāyām [(GG 267.1: Śrāyantīyam)],

5 r r 5
tarobhir vo vidā4d vāsūm [(GG 237.4: Dhānākam II), and]

5 r r 5
purojitī vo4 'ṃdhāsāḥ [(GG 545.6: Āndhīgavam)].

21. The fourth [*mudrā* ascends] to the third [*mudrā*, as in the excerpts] *dūtam, devo,* [and] *mānā*.

Commentary:

[Examples of *pratyutkrama* from 4 to 3 include]

5r 4
dūtā3ṃ [(GG 12.1: Vaiśvamanasam)],

5r 4
devo3 [(GG 55.1: Draviṇam), and]

5r 4
mānā3 [(GG 128.2: Tānvam II)].

Tā, vo, and *nā:* these syllables [from the above extracts] are illustrations [of *pratyutkrama* from 4 to 3]. Here the *svara*s of the fourth [*mudrā*] ascend to [those of] the third [*mudrā*].

22. The third [*mudrā* ascends] to the second [*mudrā*, as] in [the excerpt] *hiṣī*, and so on.

Commentary:

[An example of *pratyutkrama* from 3 to 2 is]

3 5
hī234ṣī [(GG 1.1: Gautamasya Parkaḥ)].

Here, [on] the utterance *hī,* the third [*mudrā*] ascends to the second [*mudrā*].

23. The second [*mudrā* ascends to] the first [*mudrā*, as] in [the excerpt] *au ho agne*.

Commentary:

In [the excerpt]

2r 2r 1
au holi / agne rāthā23m [(GG 5.2: Śairīṣam)]

the utterance *ho* ascends from the *svara* of the second [*mudrā*] to [that of] the first [*mudrā*].

24. The low [*mudrā*], having passed over the fourth [finger], ascends to the third [*mudrā*, as] in the euphonically joined [extract] *pāvne*.

मन्द्रश्चतुर्थतृतीयावतिक्रम्य द्वितीयं प्रत्युत्क्रामति ''षिभाभिप्रि'' ।।२५।।

मन्द्रश्चतुर्थतृतीयस्वरावतिक्रम्य द्वितीयस्वरं प्रत्युत्क्रामति। ''षिभा२ उ३। वा३४५'' (ग्रा.गा. १६.९.५५४.२) इति भकारः। ''ए५। अभि प्रिया २'' (ग्रा.गा. १६.९.५५४.२) इति ग्राशब्दः [च] मन्द्रात् द्वितीयं प्रत्युत्क्रामति ।।२५।।

तृतीयो द्वितीयमतिक्रम्य प्रथमं प्रत्युत्क्रामति ''पुनानायाम्'' ।।२६।।

''पुना ३१'' (ग्रा.गा. १४.५.५११.१६)। अयं यौधाजये ।।२६।।

चतुर्विधोऽतिक्रमः मो षुत्वा-रोहन्-यज्ञादीनि। त्र्यन्तरोऽश्विनोर्व्रते ।।२७।।

क्रुष्टः प्रथममतिक्रामति। ''ऊ २। न ओ गा २३४ ही'' (ग्रा.गा. ७.६.२८४.२) ओषुत्वा साम्नि ।।२८।।

प्रथमो द्वितीयम्। ''आरोऽ३हां'' आरोहन् साम्नि ।।२९।।

तृतीयश्चतुर्थं। ''यज्ञा५य'' साम्नि (ग्रा.गा. १.४.३५.४) ।।३०।।

प्रथमस्त्रीनतिक्रामति-अश्विनोर्व्रते। ''ई५ही हीही ही हि'' (आ.गा. १८१) अश्वि-नोर्व्रते साम्नि ।।३१।।

चतुः प्रकारोऽतिक्रमो भवति। यथा- ''मोषु त्वा'' याम् (ग्रा.गा. ७.६.२८४.२) ऊकारः क्रुष्टात् द्वितीयमागच्छति। ''आरो३हा'' (ग्रा.गा. ३.१०.९२.१) इत्यत्र 'रो' शब्दः प्रथमात् तृतीयमागच्छति। ''यज्ञऽ५य'' (ग्रा.गा. १.४.३५.४) इति 'ज्ञा' शब्दः तृतीयान्मन्द्रं याति। त्रीन् स्वरान् (तरन्नायाति) त्र्यन्तरः। यथा
तंताइयति, अन्तरायति
''अश्विनोर्व्रते'' साम्नि। अ [ति] क्रमणोदाहरणानि प्रमाणो (प) ज्ञातानि ।।३१।।

Commentary:

Taking euphonic combination [(*saṇdhi*)] into account,

43r 4 5r r 3r 2 3 5
sunota somapā / āvnā o234 vā [(GG 285.2: Gaurīvitam II)

is an example of *pratyutkrama* from 5 to 3]. Here the utterance *pā* ascends from the low [*mudrā*] to the third [*mudrā*].

25. The low [*mudrā*], having passed over the fourth and third [fingers], ascends to the second [*mudrā*, as in the excerpts] *ṣibha* [and] *bhi pri.*

Commentary:

The low [*mudrā*], having passed over *svaras* of the fourth and third [*mudrā*s], ascends to a *svara* of the second [*mudrā*]. The syllable *bhā* [of the extract]

4 5 111
ṣibhā2u / vā345 [(GG 559.2: Yāmam II)

is an example of *pratyutkrama* from 5 to 2]. [In the extract]

4 4 5
e5 / abhi priyā2̂ [(GG 554.2: Aiḍaṃ Kāvam)]

the utterance *yā* exhibits ascent from the low [*mudrā*] to the second [*mudrā*].

26. The third [*mudrā*], having passed over the second [*mudrā*], ascends to the first [*mudrā*, as] in [the extract] *punānā.*

Commentary:

[An example of *pratyutkrama* from 3 to 1 is the excerpt]

3 2 2
punā31 / nā3̂ḥ [(GG 511.16)].

This [excerpt occurs] in the Yaudhājaya [-*sāman*].

27. There are four kinds of *atikrama* [("omission"), found in *sāmans* beginning with the words] *mo ṣu tvā, ārohan, yajñā* and so on. [And] in [the first] aśvinor vratam [chant of the āraṇyakagāna] three intervening [*svaras*] are omitted.

28. The *kruṣṭa* [*mudrā*] omits the first [*mudrā* in crossing to the second *mudrā*, as in the extract] *ū na ā gāhī.*

29. The first [*mudrā* omits] the second [*mudrā* in crossing to the third *mudrā*, as in the extract] *ārohān.*

30. The third [*mudrā* omits] the fourth [*mudrā* in crossing to the fifth *mudrā* , as in the extract] *yajñāya.*

31. The first [*mudrā*] omits three [successive *mudrās* in crossing to the fifth *mudrā*, as] in [the first] aśvinor vratam [*sāman*, which has the passage] *ī hī hī hī hī hi.*

पञ्चविधं कर्षणम्। आद्वितीयकर्षणमातृतीयकर्षणमाचतुर्थकर्षणमामन्द्रकर्षणम्। मन्द्रश्चातिस्वार्यात् कृष्यते। "बोधा२" (ग्रा.गा. १.२.१५.१)। "ओऽ२३इन्द्रो" (ग्रा. ७.५.२७५.२) "न्माऽ२३४भाइ" (ग्रा.गा. २.८.८७.१)। "ओऽ२३४५इ" (ग्रा.गा. १.१.३.१)। "त्वं न्त्वाऽ६मे" (ग्रा.गा. २.४.४२.२) ।।३२।।

मन्द्रश्चातिस्वार्यात् कृष्यत इति। तावत् कृष्यते यावदतिस्वारे अनुमानेऽप्येवमेव भविष्यति।
मन्द्रश्च आ अति
स्वरस्य अन्यस्याधारत्वाभावात् तत्र व्याप्तं सदेव ध्रुवम्। अन्येषां स्वराणां सर्वेषु स्वरेषु कर्षणं प्राप्तं दर्शयति।
अन्यस्याधारत्वादभावात्
यथा जराबोधीये "बोधाऽ २"। कावषे "आर२३न्द्राः। विशोविशीये "न्मा २३४भाइ"। "अग्निं दूतं" इत्यत्र "ओ २३४५इ"। "मुड्डा" (गौतमे ★)। त्वं त्वाद्मे ।।३२।।

इति मात्रालक्षलणे सविवरणे प्रथमा खण्डिका समाप्ता ।।१।।

★ उद्वया में इत्यत्र उदाहरणं घटते। "मुड्डा" इति उदाहरणं नोपलभ्यते।

Commentary:

Atikrama is of four types. Accordingly, in [the chant beginning] *mo ṣu tvā* the letter *ū* reaches the second [*mudrā*] from the *kruṣṭa* [*mudrā*, as illustrated in the excerpt 11 3 5

ū2̂ / na ā^ gā234hī (GG 284.2: Ātram II)].

[In the extract] 1r S 2

āro3hān [(GG 92.1: Ārūḍhavad Āṅgirasaṃ Yāmaṃ Vā)]

the syllable *ro* reaches the third [*mudrā*] from the first [*mudrā*].

[In the extract] 4 3

yajñā5ya [(GG 35.4: Yajñāyajñīyam)]

the syllable *jñā* moves from the third [*mudrā*] to the low [*mudrā*].

"The three intervening [*svaras*" mentioned in rule 27 refers to] the [group of] three *svaras* that comes between [the *svaras* of the first and fifth *mudrās*]. For instance, [this occurs] in the [first] Aśvinor Vratam chant, [in the extract

1 1 2r 3r 2

ī5 hī hī hī hī hi (ĀrG 103.1].

The [above] examples of omitting [*mudrās*/*svaras*] were discovered through authoritative perception.

32. There are five kinds of *karṣaṇa*: [they are] *karṣaṇa* to the [*svaras* of the] second, third, fourth, and low [*mudrās*]; also, [a *svara* of] the low [*mudrā*] is extended on account of the *atisvāra* [*mudrā*]. [Examples of the five cases are] *bodhā, āindrāḥ, nmābhāi, oi,* [and] *tvan tvām e.*

Commentary:

[The statement] "also, [a *svara* of] the low [*mudrā*] is extended on account of the *atisvārya* [*mudrā*" needs clarification]. It is extended as long as [that nasalization] on the *atisvāra* [*mudrā*]. On reflection, moreover, it will be [performed] exactly in this manner. [There is no *karṣaṇa*] of the remaining *svara* [(that is, of the *atisvārya*)] due to the absence of a subsequent lower [*mudrā*]. [Its] mere existence is immutable. Of the other *svaras*, it is shown [that] *karṣaṇa* is found on all [of these] *svaras*. For instance, in the [first] Jarābodh [īyam chant]:

1

bodhā2 [(GG 15.1)];

[in the second Kāvaṣam chant]: 1 2

ā23indrāḥ [(GG 275.2)];

in the Viśoviśīyam: 1

nmā234bhāi [(GG 87.1)];

[in the chant beginning with the words] *agniṃ dūtam*:

1

o2345i [(GG 3.1: Bṛhad Bhāradvājam)];

[in the Gautamam]: 5 5

tvan tvā6m e [(GG 42.2)].

द्वितीया खण्डिका

त्रिविधः स्वारः प्रथमादिर्द्वितीयादिस्तृतीयादिरिति ।।१।।

वर्तिष्यते त्रिप्रकारः ।।१।।

प्रथमादिर्नवमात्रः । द्वितीयादिः षण्मात्रः । तृतीयादिरष्टमात्रः । ''हरीऽ३श्रीऽ२३४५:'' (ग्रा.गा. ९.५.१९५.१) । ''रयाऽ३४५यिम्'' (ग्रा.गा. १.३.२२.१) ''ईऽ२३४५''

इम्

(आ.गा. ४७) ।।२।।

''हरिश्रीः'' अयं नवमात्रः । ''रयायिम्'' अयं षण्मात्रः । वैराजनिधने ''ई२३१११'' इत्यष्टमात्रः ।।२।।

यन्मन्द्रद्वितीयतृतीयैः स्वरैरकृष्टं प्रत्युत्क्रामति अनन्तरोच्चे प्रत्यये तद्द्विमात्रादिः ।।३।।

यन्मन्द्रतृतीयद्वितीयैः

''विस्वरमक्षरं स्वरे स्वरे त्रिमात्रं भवति'' (मा.ल. १.१६) इत्येवं प्राप्तस्य प्रतिषेधः । पदमक्षरं मन्द्रद्वितीयतृतीयैः स्वरैर्वर्तमानमकृष्टं प्रत्युत्क्रामतिं । अनन्तरे स्वरे उच्चे प्रत्यये तद्द्विमात्रादिर्भवति ।।३।।

यथा ''श्रायन्तस्तरोभिः'' ''पुरोहीष्या'' दिः । वैराजनिधनम् ''औ हो अग्न'' इति ।।४।।

तत्र निदर्शनार्थमुदाहरणानि वर्तिष्यन्ते । यथा ''श्रायन्त इवसू४रा३याम्३'' (ग्रा.गा. ७.४.२३७.१) ''तरोभिर्वो विदा४द्व३सूम्'' (ग्रा.गा. ६.१.२६७.४) । ''पुरोजिती वों ३२ . धासाः (ग्रा.गा. १६.८.५४५.६) । ''ही२३३४षी'' (ग्रा.गा. १.१.५.१) द्विमात्रिको भवति । वैराजनिधने ईकारः । औ हो३इ२ । अग्ने रा३था३३म्

''हीष्यादिः''

१राथा २.३

(ग्रा.गा. १.१.५.२) ।४।।

CHAPTER 2

1. **There are three types of *svāra* [("having musical sound"): those] beginning with the first, second, and third [numerals].**

2. **[That] beginning with the first [numeral] has a duration of nine [*mātrās*]. [That] beginning with the second [numeral] has a duration of six [*mātrās*]. [That] beginning with the third [numeral] has a duration of eight [*mātrās*]. [Examples of the three types are] *hariśrīḥ, rayim,* [and] *ī.***

Commentary:

Hariśrīḥ: this [example of *svāra*] has a duration of nine [*mātrās*]. *Rayim*: this [example of *svāra*] has a duration of six [*mātrās*]. The *nidhana.*

3 111
ī2345

of the [Mahā]vairājam [chant] has a duration of eight [*mātrās*].

3. **When [a syllable] with *svaras* [of the] low, second, or third [*mudrās*] ascends, without *karṣaṇa* [(that is, without an intervening *mudrā*)], to the next higher [*mudrā*], then the first [*svara*] is worth two *mātrās*.**

Commentary:

"A syllable divorced from accentuation has triple measure on every *svara*" [(ML 1.16)]. Therefore, this is an exception to the preceding rule. A word syllable with *svaras* [of the] low, second, and third [*mudrās*] proceeds upwards, moving without *karṣaṇa*. [Proceeding] immediately to the *svara* [of the] next higher [*mudrā*, the syllable] begins with a two-*mātrā* [*svara*].

4. **For example, on *śrayantas, tarobhiḥ, puro,* the beginning of *hiṣī,* the *vairājanidhana,* and *au ho agne.***

Commentary:

For the sake of illustration, examples are found there:
for instance,

5r 5
śrāyanta iva sū4rāyām [(GG 267.1: Śrāyantīyam)],
5 r r 5
tarobhir vo vidā4d vāsūm [(GG 237.4: Dhānākam II), and]
5 r r 5
purojitī vo4 'ṃdhāsāḥ [(GG 545.6: Āndhīgavam)].

The beginning of *hiṣī* [(GG 1.1: Gautamasya Parkaḥ)] is worth two *mātrās*, [as

न- घ्नतावामा गायत्रे चावनर्दे ।।५।।

३ २ ३र २
"यन्मन्द्रद्वितीयतृतीयैः स्वरैः" (मा.ल. २.३) इति सिद्धस्य प्रतिप्रसवः "घ्नता ३४ वामा २" (ग्रा.गा.
प्रतिसतः
८.८.३०५.१)। "अभि देवाँ ्इया २२१२" (अ.गा.प्रा. ११) ।।५।।

पाव्ने द्विमात्रौ मन्द्रतृतीयौ ।।६।।

"सुनोत सोमपाव्ना" (ग्रा.गा. ८.६.२८५.२)। अत्र [संधिवत्] कृत्वा शाखान्तरीयस्योदाहरणम् ।।६।।
सत्वं नं

ह्रस्वो मन्द्रो-अच्छा उ वा याम् ।।७।।
मन्द्रो ह्रस्वो

५ १ १ १
अच्छा२उ वाऽ३४५। विस्वरमक्षरमिति प्राप्तस्य प्रतिषेधः। "अच्छा उवा" मिति मृजन्ति ।।७।।
अच्छा मृजन्ति

दीर्घकर्षणे द्विमात्रौ प्रथमद्वितीयौ — प्रप्रा ।।८।।

१ वि र
प्रथमद्वितीयौ स्वरौ दीर्घौ भवतः। "प्र प्रा२ऽवयम्" (ग्रा.गा. १.४.३४.१) ।।८।।

द्वितीयतृतीयौ च — भरतायत्सोमे; नर्यो३ ।।९।।

१· २र २ र र २ र
"भरताऽ३यत्सोमे३" (ग्रा.गा. ५.८.१८८.१)। "नर्यो३" (ग्रा.गा. १४.५.५१२.२)।। द्वितीयतृतीययोश्च स्वरयोर्यद् दीर्घकर्षणं तस्मिंश्च तौ द्वितीयतृतीयौ स्वरौ [भवतः] ।।९।।

is the beginning of *ho* in *au hoi agne rāthām*] [(GG 5.2: Śairīṣam)]. On the *vairājanidhana* the vowel *ī* [begins with a two-*mātrā svara*]. [In]

2r 2r 1
au holi / agne rāthā23m [(GG 5.2: Śairīṣam)
the syllable *ho* begins with a two-*mātrā* svara].

5. [The rule is] not [valid in the passage] *ghnatāvām ā* and in the *avanarda*[*na*] of the gāyatram.

Commentary:

[The rule beginning] "when [a syllable] with *svaras* [of the] low, second, or third [*mudrās*" (ML 2.3)] is not applicable [to]

3 2 3r . 2
ghnatā34vām āl [(GG 305.1: Aśvinoḥ Saṃyojanam)].

[Neither is it applicable to]

2 1 r r 2
abhi devāṁ iyā1212 [(Gāyatram: from the *retasyā* or "semen" verse of the *bahiṣpavamānastuti*)].

6. On *pāvne* [the *svaras* of] the low and third [*mudrās*] are worth two *mātrās* each.

Commentary:

[In the extract

43r 4 5r r 3r 2
sunota somapā / āvnā [(GG 285.2: Gaurīvitam II)]

the syllable *pā* is split between two *parvans*]. Carrying out euphonic combination here is a characteristic of another Vedic school.

7. [In the excerpt] *accha u vā* the low [*mudrā*] is short.

Commentary:

This [too] is an exception to the rule "a syllable divorced from accentuation [has triple measure on every *svara*]." [The passage in question] is *accha u vā.*

8. In *dīrghakarṣaṇa* [("extension of a long [syllable]")] both the first and second [*mudrās* have *svaras*] worth two *mātrās* each, [as in the excerpt] *praprā.*

Commentary:

The *svaras* [of the] first and second [*mudrās*] are long. [An example of this is the extract] *praprā vayam.*

9. [In *dīrghakarṣaṇa*] both the second and third [*mudrās*] also [have *svaras* worth two *mātrās* apiece, as in the excerpts] *bharatā, yat some,* [and] *naryo.*

Commentary:

[Examples of this are]

1 2r
bharatā3 [(GG 98.2: Prahitaḥ II)],

स्वारे त्रयोऽन्त्याः पृथगेकमात्राः ।।१०।।

स्वारे त्रयः स्वराः [द्वि] तीयादयः पृथगेकमात्रा भवन्ति ।।१०।।
स्वारौ त्रयः स्वरातीयादयः

ह्रस्वकर्षणे पृथङ्मात्रिकौ स्वरौ। ''सुवितम्; तुरय; सहस्रधारम्'' ।।११।।

सुवितऽ३म् । यस्यको ना'' (ग्रा.गा. ८.९.३१६.२) । ''तुरयऽ१ । तो हविन्ता इ'' (ग्रा.गा. ९.११.३३७.१) । ''सहस्रधारर२म्'' (ग्रा.गा. १७.११.५८१.६) इति ।।११।।

त्रिविधोद्घातो — व्यदा-मतौ-ऋचौ हो-प्रभृतीनि ।।१२।।

उद्घातः त्रिप्रकारो भवति । ''व्यदातोयाऽ२इ'' (ग्रा.गा. १.१.१.१); ''मतौऽ२हुवाइ'' (ग्रा.गा. ३.२.१२८.२) ''ऋचौऽ२हो'' (ग्रा.गा. ३.५.४८.२) ।।१२।।

पञ्चस्वरैर्युक्तं धार्यम्। ''गृणानोह'' (ग्रा.गा. १.१.१.३); ''द्रविणस्युर्विपन्यया२'' (ग्रा.गा. १.१.४.२); ''विपां ज्योताइ'' (ग्रा.गा. ३.११.९८.१); ''आदित् प्रत्नाऽ५स्य रेतसाः'' (ग्रा.गा. १.२.२०.१); ''अग्निं वो वृधान्ताम्'' (ग्रा.गा. १.३.२१.१) ।।१३।।

[पञ्चस्वरैः] संयुक्तं धार्यम् । गृणानो ह । अत्र णकारो धार्यः प्रथमस्वरे । द्रविणस्युर्विपन्यया । अत्र विशब्द-णशब्दौ धार्यौ द्वितीयस्वरे । विपां ज्योता३यि । अत्र ज्योशब्दः तृतीयस्वरे । ''आदित्प्रत्नास्यरेतसा'' इति दित्र [त्नौ] धार्यौ चतुर्थस्वरे । अग्निं वो वृधांताम् । अत्र वोवृधा इत्येतानि त्रीणि मन्द्रस्वरे । एवमादि सर्वत्र द्रष्टव्यम् ।।१३।।

2 r r
yat some3 [(GG 188.1: Vaitahavyam), and]
2 r
naryo3 [(GG 512.13: Guddaḥ)].

Also, when there is *dīrghakarṣaṇa* of the *svaras* of the second and third [*mudrās*], these *svaras* [are worth two *mātrās* each].

10. On *svāra* [syllables] the last three [numbers] are worth one *mātrā* each.

Commentary:

On *svāra* [syllables] three *svaras*, beginning with [that of] the third [numeral], are worth one *mātrā* each.

11. In *hrasvakarṣaṇa* [("extension of a short [syllable]")] each of the two *svaras* has one *mātrā*, [as in the excerpts] *suvitam*, *turaya*, [and] *sahasradhāram*.

Commentary:

[Examples of *hrasvakarṣaṇa* are]

2
suvita3m [(GG 316.2: Partham II)],
2
turaya3 [(GG 337.1: Gṛtsamadasya Madaḥ I), and]
2 1 r
sahasradhāra2m [(GG 581.6: Kaulmalabarhiṣīyam III)].

12. There are three types of elevation, [as in the extracts] *vyadā*, *matau*, *ṛcau ho*, and so on.

Commentary:

Elevation is of three kinds. [Examples are]

2 1
vyadātoyā2i [(GG 1.1: Gautamasya Parkaḥ)],
21 1
matau2̄ / huvāi [(GG 128.2: Tānvam II), and]
2 2
ṛcau3 ho [(GG 48.2: Bārhaduktam II)].

13. A regular [tonal] succession is to be maintained by means of the *svaras* of the five [*mudrās*]. [Examples of this continuity of *svara* are] *gṛṇāno ha*, *draviṇasyur vipanyayā*, *vipāṃ jyotāi*, *ād it pratnāsya retasāḥ*, [and] *agniṃ vo vṛdhāntām*.

Commentary:

(With the *svaras* of the five *mudrās*] continuity [of *svara*] is to be maintained.

सप्तविधार्धमात्रा। ''ओ ग्ना इ'' (ग्रा.गा. १.१.१.१); ''प्रेष्ठं वो हाउ'' (ग्रा.गा. १.१.५.३); षु प्रावो२३चा३४३:'' (ग्रा.गा. १.३.२८.१); नायक्रमी२त्। वो अग्नाया२इ'' (ग्रा.गा. १.४.३५.१); ''तियाइ३श्चौ५रा६५६न्'' (ग्रा.गा. २.७.६४.१); ''विशो विशो हुम् स्थि वो ६ अतिथाइम्'' (ग्रा.गा. २.९.८७.१)

वो६

।।१४।।

इमाः सप्त अर्धमात्रा प्रकारा भवन्ति। यथोदाहृताः ।।१४।।

प्रकारो भवति

इति मात्रालक्षणे विवरणसमन्विते द्वितीया खण्डिका ।।२।।

In *gṛṇāno ha* the syllable *ṇā* is maintained on a *svara* of the first [*mudrā*]. In *draviṇasyur vipanyayā* the syllables *vi* and *ṇa* are kept on a *svara* of the second [*mudrā*]. In *vipāṃ jyotāi* the syllable *jyo* is on a *svara* of the third [*mudrā*]. [In] *ādit pratnāsya retasāḥ* [the syllables] °*d it* and *pra* remain on the *svara* of the fourth [*mudrā*]. In *agniṃ vo vṛdhāntām* the three [syllables] *vo vṛdhā* [(?—*gniṃ vo vṛ*?) remain] on the *svara* of the low [*mudrā*]. In this manner one should discover [the appropriate *svara/mudrā*] everywhere.

14. [There are] seven ways [in which] the one-half *mātrā* [time value occurs]. [Examples are] *ognāi, preṣṭhaṃ vo hāu, ṣu prāvocāḥ, nāy akramīt, vo agnayāi, tiyāṃ cārān,* [and] *viśo viśo hum vo atithāim.*

Commentary:

These are seven contexts of the one-half *mātrā* [duration]. They are illustrated accordingly [(but see the ensuing notes for the notation)].

।। तृतीया खण्डिका ।।

द्विविधा गतिरिगतिरुगतिश्च।
कण्ठ्योष्ठ्या कण्ठ्यतालव्या ।।१।।
कण्ठतालव्या

द्विप्रकारा गतिर्भवति। आउ इति कण्ठ्योष्ठ्या। आइ इति कण्ठ्यतालव्या ।।१।।
कण्ठतालव्या

तयोर्मात्राकालः अर्धमात्रा मात्रा वा [इति] गार्ग्यश्चाचार्यो ब्रवीति। षण्मात्राः सामिके भवन्ति। मात्रिकश्च द्विमात्रिकश्च त्रिमात्रिकश्चार्धमात्रिकश्चाध्यर्धमात्रिकश्चाणुमात्रिकश्च संपाद्या भवन्ति। यः संपादयते स आचार्यः। स च स्वरविशेषेण सामगो भवति। स्वरस्याष्टादशदोषान् प्रच्छादयति ।।२।।

गत्या उपधायाः न समानपरिमाणं भवति। किं तर्हि ? पृथग्भवति। ''दीर्घे वृद्धे चोपधौ'' (मा.ल. १.१५) इत्यत्रोक्तत्वात्। ततस्तदुच्यते अर्धमात्रा मात्रा वेति विकल्पः। ''आयाही वोयि-ना गतिरत्न'' इति स्वरमध्य आगतानां मात्रिकः कालः। वर्णान्तरेणोच्चारणात् व्यञ्जनवदर्धमात्रिक इत्येवं विकल्पः। अन्ये पुनर्व्यञ्जनान्ते
पुनर्व्यञ्जननं
[स्वरं] म [न्य] न्ते। यः व्यञ्जनकार्यं भुज्यते सः (य) अर्धमात्रिकः। यथा अतिहार [परक] इकारश्च
यः अतिहार प्रक
[यकारो] भवतीत्यत्र अर्धमात्रिकः ।।२।।
यः अतो

स्वरितविनतप्रणतोत्स्वरिताभिगीतानाम् आर्चिकोऽक्षरकालः ।।३।।

स्वरितग्रहणमाशङ्कानिवृत्त्यर्थम्। अदीर्घं दीर्घवत्कुर्यादित्युक्तम्। तेन स्वरिते यः कालपरिमाणः तथैव अत्र
वक्तुयादित्यु क्तम् स्वारितो णं अस्व
स्वरितोऽपि स्यादिति। अन्ये पुनरेवं पठन्ति। ''विनतप्रणतोत्स्वरिताभिगीतानामार्चिकोऽक्षरकालो'' भवति। न ''विस्वरमक्षरम्'' (मा.ल. १.१६) इत्यनेन यो विहितः ।।३।।

CHAPTER 3

1. There are two types of *gati, i-gati* and *u-gati.* [The two types consist of] glottal-labial and glottal-palatal [vowel combinations].

Commentary:

Gati is of two kinds. [The vowel combination] *āu* [involves] glottal and labial [sounds, whereas] *āi* [combines] glottal and palatal [sounds].

2. There is *mātrā* measurement of the two [types]. [*Gati* is worth either] one or one-half *mātrā*: thus says Gārgya, the learned teacher. In the *sāman* chant six *mātrā* [measurements] are realized: one, two, three, one-half, one and one-half, and one-quarter *mātrās*. The learned man [(*ācārya*)] is the one who brings this about; and it is the Sāmavedic chanter who distinguishes one *svara* from another. [He] conceals the eighteen transgressions of *svara*.

Commentary:

[Syllables] having the addition of *gati* are not of the same duration. Why, then, [is this so]? [*Gati*] is [measured] separately. "On [its] addition to long and augmented [syllables" (ML 1.15)] has [previously] been spoken of here. Therefore, the option "one-half *mātra* or one *mātrā*" is put forth. [*Gati* introduced by a semivowel, which occurs] between the vowels of [syllables having such] additions, has a time value of one *mātrā*, [as is the case with the] *gati* accompanying *ā yāhī voyi* [(GG 1.1)]. [The semivowel has a specific duration] due to [its] pronunciation between letters. Like a consonant, [it is worth] one-half *mātrā*: thus [the one-*mātrā*] option [for *gati*]. Moreover, it is considered [the duration] of the other consonant [(that is, the consonant that begins the syllable)]. Wherever a consonant is utilized, the one-half *mātrā* [duration results]. Accordingly, to prevent jumping over to the vowel *i* from [a preceding vowel, the letter *y*, lasting] one-half *mātrā*, [is inserted] here.

3. The time value of *ārcika* syllables [is also that] of the *svarita* [accent], *vinata* [("downwardly inclined")], *praṇata* [("respectfully saluted," "bowed in reverence")], *utsvarita* [("sounded from afar," "sounded upwards")], and *abhigīta* [("sung out, to, or over"?)].

Commentary:

On account of tempo [(rhythm?)] there are apprehensions [connected with]

विनतं प्रथमादिर्द्वितीयान्तम्। द्वितीयादिस्तृतीयान्तं प्रणतम्। उत्स्वरितं चतुर्थादिर्मन्द्रान्तम्। अभिगीतं द्वितीयादिः प्रथमान्तम् ।।४।।

विनतं प्रथमस्वरादि [द्वितीयस्वरान्तम्।] द्वितीयस्वरादिस्तृतीयस्वरान्तं प्रणतम्। चतुर्थस्वरादिर्मन्द्रस्वरान्तम् [उत्स्वरितम्]। अभिगीतं द्वितीयस्वरादिः प्रथमस्वरान्तम् ।।४।।

विनतप्रणतयोरन्त्येऽर्धमात्रा नीचेन स्वरेण भवति। उच्चेऽध्यर्धा। दीर्घे ह्रस्वेऽर्द्धम्। "यं यं यं २ म् याम्" (ग्रा.गा. ११.३३७.२)। स्ये बहुलं संमील्ये; "पिबा सोमम्" (ग्रा.गा. १०.५.३९८.१); "अभीनवन्ते" (ग्रा.गा. १६.८.५५०); "उदुब्रह्माणि" (ग्रा.गा. ८.१०.३३०)। "इन्द्रस्य नु वीर्याणि" (सा. ६१२); "कश्यपपुच्छे; महादिवाकीर्त्ये; आनन्दे" (आ.गा. २७१)। आया हि ३वोई। तिग्मेना ३शो। मन्ये३। शुक्रियेषु ओषधीना३म् ।।५।। आयाहिऽ१वो३इ। तिग्मेन१शोऽ३। रम्मन्येदाऽ३। शुक्रियेषु — "ओऽ२ष धीऽ२नाऽ२म्" ।।५।।

विनतप्रणतयोरन्तेऽर्धमात्रा नीचेन स्वरेण भवति। उच्चे स्वरे अध्यर्धा। तत्रोक्तो निर्णयः। विनतं [प्रथमादिर्] द्वितीयान्तम्। [द्वितीयादिस्तृतीयान्तं] प्रणतम् इति। तयोर्विनतप्रणतयोः उच्चे स्वरे अध्यर्धा भवति दीर्घे अक्षरे। ह्रस्वे तु अक्षरे उच्चेऽपि स्वरे अर्धमात्रा। "यं यं य २ याम्" "यं वृत्रेषु" (सा. ३३७) इत्यत्र विनतोदाहरणम्। स्येबहुलम् उदाहरणं संगील्ये प्रयच्चक्रमराव्णे। उदुऽ१, उदोवा, इन्द्रँऽ१, इन्द्रँऽ१,इन्द्रम् इद्रं उदुऽ१, उदु द्रं द्रं द्रो वा। कश्यपपुच्छे — व्याप्राचामिति। ऐ हीर। ऐ ही २ (आ.गा. २४८) महादिवाकीर्त्ये। तवश्यावीये — ह ँवं वरम्ऽ१ वं वम्ऽ१वम् (आ.गा. २६४), आनन्दे — उवीऽ१उवीऽ१ (आ.गा. २७२)। प्रणतोदाहरणानि। प्रमाणं प्रक्षोनामि ।।५।।

प्रणतोदाहरणानि — आयाहि, तिग्मेन, रम्मन्ये, ओषधीनाम् — (शुक्रियेषु) इत्येतानि दत्तानि।

employing the *svarita* [accent]. "One should perform [syllables that are] not long like [those that] are," it is said. "Because of that [very circumstance] on *svarita* [syllables, this accent], therefore, should turn out exactly as just stated [in the previous sentence] as far as time measurement is concerned [(i.e., short syllables should possess the value of long syllables)]." However, on the remaining [accents the Brāhmaṇs] definitely recite [rather than chant]. The time value of *ārcika* syllables is [also that] of *vinata, praṇata, utsvarita,* and *abhigīta.* It is not the "syllable divorced from accent" [(ML 1.16)] that is furnished with this [time value].

4. ***Vinata* begins with the first [finger] and ends with the second [finger]. *Praṇata* begins with the second [finger] and ends with the third [finger]. *Utsvarita* begins with the fourth [finger] and ends with the low [finger]. *Abhigīta* begins with the second [finger] and ends with the first [finger].**

Commentary:

Vinata begins with a *svara* of the first [finger] and concludes with a *svara* of the second [finger]. Beginning with a *svara* of the second [finger] and ending with a *svara* of the third [finger] is *praṇata.* Beginning with a *svara* of the fourth [finger] and ending with a *svara* of the low [finger is *utsvarita*]. *Abhigīta* begins with a *svara* of the second [finger] and ends with a *svara* of the first [finger].

5. **One-half *mātrā* occurs with the low *svara* at the end of *vinata* and *praṇata.* One and one-half [*mātrā* is found] on the high [*svara*]. [This occurs] on a long [syllable]: on a short [syllable the high *svara* is worth] one-half [*mātrā*]. [An example is] *yaṃ yaṃ yaṃ yām.* In the rahasyagāna [these time values occur] many times. The two saṃmīlyam [*sāmans*], *pibā somam, abhī navante, ud u brahmāṇi, indrasya nu vīryāṇi,* the kaśyapapuccham, the mahādivākīrtyam, the *ānandaḥ, ā yāhi, tigme, ram manye,* [and] *oṣadhīnām* in the *śukriyas* [also have examples].**

Commentary:

One-half *mātrā* is found with the low *svara* at the end of *vinata* and *praṇata.* One and one-half *mātrā* is found on the high *svara.* Therefore [what is] stated is a deduction. *Vinata* [begins with the first finger] and concludes with the second [finger]. "*Praṇata* begins with the second [finger] and ends with the third [finger" (ML 3.4)]. One and one-half [*mātrā*] occurs on the upper *svara* of both *vinata* and *praṇata.* [This takes place] on a long syllable. But on a short syllable one-half *mātrā* occurs on that very upper *svara.* [The extract]

2 1 ऽ 1
yaṃ yaṃ ya2ṃ yām [(GG 337.2: Gṛtsamadasya Madaḥ II),

from a *sāman* on the *ṛc* beginning] *yaṃ vṛtreṣu,* is an example of *vinata.* In the

उत्स्वरितेऽर्धमात्रा चतुर्थे। मन्द्रेऽध्यर्धा। म[५]नुष्ये[४र]५भिः। क[४५र]ईं व्यँ[४]१क्ताँ[४]३ः ।।६।।

"मनुष्येऽ५भिरग्निः" (ग्रा.गा. २.२.१७); "कईं व्यऽ२क्ताः" (ग्रा.गा. ११.९.४३३.१)। उत्स्वरिते अर्धमात्रा चतुर्थस्वरे भवति। मन्द्रेऽध्यर्धा। मनुष्येऽ२ भिरिति। अथ कुतोऽयमार्चिकोऽक्षरकालः इत्येतस्मादेव 'कईं व्यक्ता' यां न भविष्यति। अथ कस्मात् प्रतिषेध उच्यते। उत्स्वरितपरिसंख्यानार्थं तु त.एव उत्स्वरिते भवत इति। इतरथा ऋक्स्वरवदित्यत्रोक्तत्वात् 'उच्चमुच्चेन नीचं नीचेन' इति। अन्यत्रापि स प्रायेण। "पूर्वाणि स्वरितसंयोगात्" इत्यतो न "कयींव्यक्ता" इत्युक्तम्। मनुष्येभिः कईं व्यक्ताः ।।६।।

हविष्मद्भिः

अभिगीतेऽ र्धमात्रा द्वितीये। प्रथमेऽध्यर्धा। स्तोमां रुद्रापिन्वो अर्कैः ।।७।।

Rahasyagāna it is seen many times. Example[s] [occur] in the Saṃmīlyam, [on the ṛc beginning] *pra yac cakram arāvṇe.* (Other examples are]

1 ᵕ 1 ᵕ 1 2 1r r
udu2 / udu2 / udu / ud o vā [(ĀrG 114.2: Vasiṣṭhavratam II) and]
2 1ᵕ 1S 1 2 1r r
indra2m / indra2m / indram / indro vā [(ĀrG 114.2: Vasiṣṭhavratam II)].

[The *stobha*]

1rᵕr 1rᵕr
aihī2 aihī2 [(ĀrG 147.1)]

is scattered throughout the Kaśyapapuccham [The excerpt]

2 1 ᵕ 1 ᵕ 1
haṁ vam ya2ṃ vaṃ va2ṃ vam [(ĀrG *stobha*, after 155.1:6)

occurs] in the Mahādivākīrtyam and in the Tavaśyāvīyam [(ĀrGP)].

[The extract]

1 ᵕ 1 ᵕ
uvi2 uvi2 [(ĀrG 160.1)

is found] in the Ānandaḥ. . . . .

6. On *utsvarita* [syllables] one-half *mātrā* [occurs] on the fourth [*mudrā*]. One and one-half [*mātrā* is found] on the low [*mudrā*]. [Examples are] *manuṣyebhiḥ* and *ka īṃ vyaktāḥ*.

Commentary:

[Examples of *utsvarita* are]

5 4r 4
manuṣye5bhir agniḥ [GG 79.1: Prāsāham) and]
4 5r 4. 4
ka īṃ vya5ktāḥ [(GG 433.1: Hikam)].

On *utsvarita* [syllables] one-half *mātrā* occurs on the *svara* of the fourth [*mudrā*]. One and one-half [*mātrā* occurs] on the low [*mudrā*]. [An example] is *manuṣyebhiḥ.* But because this [example has] "the time value of an *ārcika* syllable," for that very reason [this measurement] will not be found on *ka īṃ vyaktāḥ.* But for what reason is the exception stated? These very two [examples] with *utsvarita* are found [here] just for the sake of enumerating *utsvarita* [types]. On the other hand, because of being uttered here "like the *svara* of [the source] *ṛc*," [*utsvarita* has the characteristic] "high with the high, low with the low." Elsewhere also this is generally [true]. The former [types are so named] "because of a connection with the *svarita* [accent]," but not *ka īṃ vyaktāḥ.* [The extracts] *manuṣyebhiḥ* [and] *ka īṃ vyaktāḥ* [show two *utsvarita* varieties].

7. On *abhigīta* [syllables] one-half *mātrā* is found on the second [*mudrā*], one and one-half [*mātrā*] on the first [*mudrā*]. [Examples are] *stomaṃ rudrā* [and] *arkaiḥ*.

"स्तोमऽ ँ रुद्राऽ२३ याँ पाइन्वो अर्काऽ२३४५इः। अभिगीतेऽर्धमात्रा द्वितीये। प्रथमे अध्यर्धा दीर्घे। ह्रस्वे न च। स्तोम ँ रुद्रापिन्वो अर्कैः। एवं पाठः अभिगीते उभयोर् युज्यतैव। अर्धमात्रा द्वितीये स्वरे भवति। प्रथमे

उभये युक्यरो वा

अध्यर्धा। दीर्घे ह्रस्वे प्रथमे अध्यर्धमात्राया स्तोम ँ रुद्राह्रस्वं जनयंस्तूर्यमपि दीर्घम् ।।७।।

त्सूर्य

अभिगीतकृष्टादिरर्धमात्रा नीचेन स्वरेण भवति। उच्चेऽर्धतिस्रः। तोध्वाराइ।

अभिगीते

तोक्षरान्। इन्द्रं वृधा ४ तो २ ध्वां २३ रो इ। तो २ क्षां २३४ रो न् ।।८।।

अभिगीतात् कृष्यते [यतः] तदभिगीतकृष्टम्। तस्य अभिगीतकृष्टस्य आदिरभिगीतकृष्टादिः। अर्धमात्रापरिमाणतः नीचेन स्वरेण प्रयुज्यते। अत्रोक्तो निर्णयः। अभिगीतं द्वितीयादिरिति। प्रथमेऽर्धतिस्रो मात्रा भवन्ति। अन्ये पुनरेवं पठन्ति प्रथमस्त्रिमात्र इति। उच्यते आशङ्काविनिवृत्त्यर्थम् इन्द्रं वृधातो ।।८।।

उत्तरो यकारोऽणुमात्रो रायायाम्। रो र योया‍ऽ२३ग्ने ४ र महे र त्वा र होउ (ग्रा.गा. ३.१०.९३.२)। ऋकारादिरणुमात्रा। रेफोऽर्धमात्रा। मध्ये शेषा स्वरभक्तिरर्धमात्रा। स्थितसंधितं च। न च स्वरस्य विकारश्चेति वक्ष्यति। हरेफोष्मसंयोगे रेफपरा

विकार

स्वरभक्तिर [र्ध] मात्रा इति मात्राणुमात्राणां संपाद्यः कालः ।।९।।

अक्त मत्रा रक्त मात्रा

ऋकारस्यादिरवकृष्यते। पूर्वेण स्वरेण सहाणुमात्र उक्तः। तस्मिन्नेव ऋकारस्य स्वरोऽन्तर्भूतः।

मौतृरूक्तः स्वरान्तर्

पर्णकृणिवत्। यस्येदं परिमाणं रेफस्य व्यञ्जनं क्राकारमध्ये स तु न संबन्धीयते। पूर्वेण स्वरेण सह भिन्नजातीयत्वात्। व्यञ्जनत्वाद्रौह्यमिति च स्वरे संधेरेव विकृतः। शास्त्रान्तरे चोक्तम्। न व्यञ्जने स्वराः संधेया इति। अतः तस्येदं परिमाणं सामस्वरभक्तिः। स्वैकदेशोऽस्वरः। रेफात् परः अवशिष्यते। पूर्वेण स्वरेण समानः प्रश्लिष्टः। असावप्यर्धमात्रां (त्रः ?)। तस्य तदर्थो लोपः। न व्यञ्जने स्वराः संधेया इति। एवं चेदं (° दयं ?) यकारो विभज्यमानः अतिरिच्यते। मातृकापरिमाणात्। मात्रा हि अवशिष्टा योज्यमाना लक्षणमात्रा

मातृकात्

विवक्षितमेव स्वरवर्णनं परिकरोति। ऋकारांशः अणुमात्रो विभज्यमानो भवति। क्राकारमध्ये यो रेफः सोऽर्धमात्रो

स्वावर्णनापरिकरोदि

न भवति। शेषा स्वरभक्तिर्विक्रियमाणेऽ (णोऽ ?) र्धमात्रो न भवति। परिमाणोऽत्र यथा संध्यमयवायामित्यत्र संध्यक्षराणामिकारांशो वा यो यकारमापद्यते। यकारावस्थितं चार्धमात्रिकं भवत्यधिकारः। यस्मिंश्चकित इन्द्राद्रडा एवमादिषु मात्रार्द्धमात्रिकं [मा] त्राणुमात्रा तेन संपद्यते। कालो न शक्यते संपादयितुम् ।।९।।

Commentary:

One-half *mātrā* is found on *abhigīta* [syllables]. [This value occurs] on the second [*mudrā*]. [This is true] on either long or short [vowels, as in] *stomaṁ rudrā* [and] *apinvo arkaiḥ*. Thus the reading: on both kinds of *abhigīta* one-half *mātrā* is found on the second *svara*. On the first, one and one-half occurs. On long and short [vowels, the time value] of one and one-half *mātrā* occurs on the first: *stomaṁ rudrā* [has] the short [vowel], *janayaṃt sūryam api* the long.

8. One-half *mātrā* is found with the low *svara* at the beginning of *abhigītakṛṣṭa*. Two and one-half [*mātrā*]s occur on the high [*svara*]. [Examples are] *to dhva* [and] *to kṣa*.

Commentary:

That which is drawn from the *abhigīta* is *abhigītakṛṣṭa*. One-half *mātrā* by measure is connected with the low *svara* at the beginning of *abhigītakṛṣṭa*. The inference stated here is "*abhigīta* beginning with the second [*svara*]." Two and one-half *mātrā*s occur on the first [*svara*]. On the other hand, others teach "a three-*mātrā* first [*svara*]." [This] is prescribed for the sake of removing uncertainty—[for instance, in the extract] *indraṃ vṛdhānte*.

9. Final *y* amounts to one-quarter [*mātrā*, as in] *rāyāy*. Initial *ṛ* is worth one-quarter *mātrā*. The letter *r* is worth one-half *mātrā*. *Svarabhakti* supplied in the middle [of a word] is worth one-half *mātrā*. Also [that] standing joined [through *sandhi* is worth one-half *mātrā*]. It increases [the duration], "although not [through] vowel modification." In the conjunction of *h*, *r*, and a sibilant, the *svarabhakti* followed by [(or following] *r* [amounts to] one *mātrā* [(?), while] the complete time value of one and one-quarter *mātrās* [holds for the two sounds combined].

Commentary:

. . . The beginning of *ṛ* is discarded. One-quarter *mātrā* is uttered with [*ṛ* as] the initial vowel. Only on it [(i.e., the one-quarter *mātrā*)] is the *svara* of *ṛ* present, at the end. [It is] like a leaf-worm, [which munches on the ends of the leaves]. However, this [one-quarter *mātrā*] duration is not associated with a consonant [in conjunction] with an *r*, [which occurs, for instance,] in the middle of the syllable *krā*. [It is associated] with the initial vowel, on account of [its] being of a different species [of sound]. Due to being a consonant, [as in] *rauhyam*, modification in the sound [of the letter *r* arises] only from euphonic combination. [This] is spoken of in another *śāstra* [(see MI 1.9-10)]. "[Musical] sounds do not occur in connection with a consonant." Hence this measuring of it [relates to] Sāmavedic vowel separation [(*svarabhakti*)]. [Musical] sound occurs on the eleven vowels. The [vowel] sound following the letter *r* is a remnant. It is similar

प्रतिज्ञा खलु वर्तते। प्रतिज्ञा खलु वर्तते ।।१०।।

प्रतिज्ञामात्रा जानिहितम्। तथोक्तं शास्त्रान्तरेऽपि। तत्पुनरिदमवशिष्टम्। विश्वावस्वादयश्च गन्धर्वाः सामस्तु (सु ?) निभृतं करणं स्वरसौक्ष्मात्तेऽपि हि न कुर्युः ।।१०।।

इति मात्रालक्षणे विवरसमन्विते तृतीया खण्डिका समाप्ता ।।३।।

।। मात्रालक्षणं समाप्तम् ।।

to and coalescent with, the preceding vowel. Moreover, this [following sound] is worth one-half *mātrā*. Its purpose is elision. "[Musical] sounds do not occur in connection with consonants." Therefore *y* also, having a fractional duration, creates a surplus. [This results] from measuring the [letters of the] alphabet. Because the *mātrā* [measurement] assigns durations to the remnants, indicating *mātrā* is useful only in promoting the intended goal: [namely], the description of *svara*. The *ṛ* portion, measured by a fraction, has one-quarter *mātrā*. The [letter] *r* located in the middle of the syllable *krā* is not worth one-half *mātrā*. *Svarabhakti* resulting from the purposeful change [of final *s* to *r*] does not amount to one-half [*mātrā*]. In this instance, accordingly, duration results from euphonic combination [(i.e., the substitution of *r* for *s*); likewise], in [cases like] *ayavāy* the *i*-element of the diphthongs changes into *y* [when a vowel follows]. The prevailing rule is that fixed *y* is worth one-half *mātrā*. [A case like] *indrād-raḍāḥ*, in which trembling [is elicited, has a measurement that] amounts to one *mātrā* plus one-half *mātrā* [and] one *mātrā* [(?)] plus one-quarter *mātrā* on the beginning [letters]. Time measure is not capable of being effected [in such a case].

10. The proposition indeed is fulfilled: the proposition indeed is fulfilled.

Commentary:

The proposed statement about *mātrā* is brought to fruition. [It is] thus put forth in the very remainder of the treatise. Apart from this the following remains [to be said]: the gandharvas Viśvāvasu and so on [sought to learn] the secret time calculation present in the Sāmavedic chants; [but], due to the subtlety of *svara*, even they would not accomplish [this].

[The section of the commentary given below is found in some manuscripts and Dr. B.R. Sharma has inserted them in his edition just after Sutra-9. Since it does not go with the ninth Sutra and is rather corrupt, it has been omitted in the text. Obviously the Sutra with which this commentary should have given is itself missing in the extent manuscripts.]

अत्र वृहायोशक्र इति वृहा उपदिष्टा स्यात्तद्देशादिस्तूर्गा इति। तत्र चाशब्दो द्वितीये स्वरपरयशब्दप्रथमस्वरस्तु प्रथमस्वराय तृतीयात् कृष्यते। वाष्वभ्यां श्वान्त्यमक्षरं कृष्टं भवतीति सिद्धं सर्वपरं त्वातन्त्राक्षरस्य। तेन कृष्टादकार आकारीभूतकालातिरेकात् यकार आकारीभूतो विमुच्यते। यशब्दस्य अवायन्त्यत इति संनिकर्ष-प्रतिषेध उक्तः। तेन कृष्टत्वादकारस्य कालातिरेकत्वात् सर्वपरत्वात् कारणविहितं तस्मिन् सन्विते (संधिते ?) संनिकर्षो भवति। संनिकर्ष [इ] ति च क्रियमाणं संध्यमयवायावमित्यनेन यकारोत्पत्तिं प्राप्नोति। तत्र अनृक्संहितामित्यनेन संहिताभ्युपगम [प] क्षत इति कृत्वा येशब्दस्य विनतंनिमित्तेनैव रूपान्तरं प्राप्तो येन यकारापत्तिः स्यात्। स उच्यते। प्राप्नोति। कथम् ? त्वेशब्दस्य संध्यगीतो भवति इत्यत्रोक्तम्। त्वे अग्नि-

सिद्धिग्रहणादेकात्त्वेशब्दाच्चान्यस्य अकारं (रः ?)। आकारीभूते प्रत्यये निवृत्तिः कथं भवति? लक्षणादेव संनिकर्षं कृत्वा। तस्मिंश्च क्रियमाणे संध्यमयवायावमित्यनेन यकारो भवतीत्युपपन्नम्। तस्य परस्य मध्य इत्यनेन लोपः। लुप्तस्य व्यवस्था इत्यनेन भावी यकारः प्राप्नोति। भुक्तं पूर्वस्थानम्। भुज्यत इति भोगः। तस्य प्राप्तस्य एहाई इति प्रतिषेधः। एहाईवत्वात् पर्वणः प्रतिषेधः प्रतिषेधस्य प्रसरायार्धमिति अर्धं तु (भु) ज्यत इति व्यवस्था इत्यनेन सर्वत्रैवार्धयकारो भवति। अवशिष्टत्वाद्धेतोः मात्रार्द्धमात्रा इत्यनेन कालविकल्प उक्तो व्यञ्जनस्य। तदा [उभयं] पक्षं गृहीत्वा अर्धमात्रिकपक्षे चोपदिश्यते। उत्तरो यकारोऽणुमात्रो रायायामिति

उपवं

पूर्वतर इति नित्यं यकारो उभयत्र उच्यते। एके एवं वर्णयन्ति। अस्मदाचार्यास्तु पुनर्नैव। इकारस्य तु

मयेत्वा

वृद्धावितिरिति सत्व अत्वो नास्ति। तस्मादुक्तमेवाकारस्याकारे निवृत्तिरिति। अस्य तु तन्नोपपद्यते। वृद्ध्यादि-भिर्भावैरभिसंबन्धात्। कथं तर्हि भवति। उच्यते। बृहाणशक्र इति उपदेशादगृहायाश्चेदेस्तूरे इत्ययमुद्देशः। तेन त्रिद्व्यक्षरेषु आद्येषु वा षड्भिः शेषेषु स्तुरस्वरः। तेन राश[ब्दे], प्रथमेऽकारः प्रथमस्वरस्थः। यश[ब्दे]

राशब्दो यशब्दो

प्रथमोऽकारः प्रथमस्वरस्थः। एवं स न कृष्यते। वाष्वभ्यां तत्वाद्वाष्वद्धिः सर्वापरा सर्वयश्च कर्षणम्। नित्यकृष्टत्वात्। तेन अकार आतृतीयात् कृष्यते। महेत्वा इत्येतानि चतुर्थे स्वरे स्थितानि। हाउशब्दस्तु मन्द्रविस्वर अकृष्टत्वात्। एवं स्थिते हाशब्द [ए] वोन्नत इति वृद्धिः अकारो (रे?)। अकारेऽपि द्वितीयस्वरस्य कृष्टत्वात् कसोतुकर्षपा तृतीयाद्भवति। चतुर्थस्य प्रत्यय इत्यनेन यशब्दस्यावृत्त्यन्तरे इत्यनेन वृद्धिः। वृद्धौ सत्यां वृन्दामित्यनेनाभावः। आभूतस्य तालव्यस्य वृद्ध्या गत्यन्तता। अन्यार्थो (र्थं) गम्यते। कथं यन्ति

वृध्यात्

गतिश्चान्तस्थामापद्यत इत्यत्र सिद्धवत्तद्विविद्धायिस्वरयोरिति अधिकार इति ग्रहणशा[स्त्रे] स्त्र नोक्तम्। तदा भूतं तद्गतरेफान्तमिति। योज्यद्वितीष्टान्नंभाव इति समुच्चारणाद् वृदामित्यत्र न तद्विविद्धायिपचता पक्तायि इत्येवं प्रमाणात् प्रमाणं वभृत्संजठरे तस्माद्गत्यन्तं सिद्धा चेद्गणात्। तथा सति गतिश्चान्तस्थामापद्यते इत्यनेन यकारापत्तिः। ननु एवमप्युक्ते यकारापत्तिं प्रति संदेहश्चान्तस्थाबहुत्वात्। कः सन्देहः। कथं विकारसंस्थानेत्युक्तं चतुर्गते स्थानमसिद्धमेव। आह सिद्धम्। कथम् ? इकारेण सहैकत्वात्। यदुच्यते यस्तोत इत्यत्र स्तोता मे गोसखा इत्युदाहरणात्। अथवा इहैवान्यथा न सिद्धिः। कथम् ? आह — द्विविधा गतिरिगतिरुगतिश्च इति कण्ठ्योष्ठ्या कण्ठ्यतालव्या (मा.ल. ३.१) इति। तस्मादन्तस्थाबहुत्वेऽपि यकारमन्तरेण भवतीत्युपप-न्नम्। तालव्यादिगते इत्यदानीं (!) च मध्य इति लोपः। लुप्तस्य व्यवस्था इत्यनेन भोगः। तस्य तु प्रतिषेधो नास्त्येव। रायार्धमित्यत्र प्रतिषिद्धस्यैवार्द्धयकारे प्राप्त्यर्थमुपदिश्यते। न च तदुक्तमर्धवायकारयोर्लुम्पन्तीति। तदेतस्मिन्नेवैकस्मिन् भवति। न सर्वस्मिन्। अकारेण एतेनैतत्परिमाणादुपदिश्यते। उत्तरो यकारोऽणुमात्रो रायायामिति नित्यमवेक्ष्य यकारम् उत्तर इत्युक्तम्। ऋकारस्त्वणुमात्रिकः। कालाभिसंबन्धादेवमुच्यते। सहष इत्यत्र यत्र हिरण्य इति व्यञ्जनम्। अकारः स्वरः। तस्य तु ऋकार उत्तरः। तस्य अकारेण सह संबन्धी यस्य

संबन्धीयस्य

योगविभागः।

NOTES

CHAPTER 1

1

The ML concerns itself solely with the time measurement of musical sound *(svara).* It does not address chant construction, which is the subject of other treatises on the Sāmaveda (the Pañcavidhasūtra, for instance). The chant extracts used for illustrative purposes by the ML and its commentator are drawn from the Prakṛtigāna (the GG and the ĀrG). Only typical cases are put forth. In other words, when discussing the number sequence *utsvarita* the ML cites two examples from the Prakṛtigāna. It does not list all examples of *utsvarita* that are found in the two songbooks.

3

A. *Short Syllables*

The rule stating that syllables with short vowels are worth one *mātrā* is valid only where conjunct consonants do not follow. The T chanters increase this value to one and one-half or two *mātrās* before conjuncts and/or differently notated syllables. This modification takes place regardless of the numerical context. The T treatment of syllables with and without the ensuing conjuncts is obvious in this and the following excerpts.

Example 1 (T). 1 *mātrā* = eighth note. Gāyatram.

Note that here the first and fourth syllables contain one and one-half instead of two *mātrās*. However, on the segmented beam I have given them two *mātrās*, which may or may not be the intended duration.

Example 2 (T). 1 *mātrā* = sixteenth note. Mahāvaiśvāmitram I (GG 343.6).

The 2 notation on the last syllable of Example 2 appears to be an outwards indication that three *mātrā*s are found here : see Example 16 for an instance of $\hat{2}$ on a short vowel.

Example 3 (T). 1 *mātrā* = eighth note. Vāmadevyam (ŪG 1.1.5).

Example 4 (T). 1 *mātrā* = sixteenth note. Hārivarṇam I (GG 383.1).

Example 5 (T). 1 *mātrā* = sixteenth note. Janitram II (GG 484.2).

Notice also that a change of notation affects a preceding short syllable similarly, thus increasing its duration to two *mātrā*s in these T renditions.

Example 6 (T). 1 *mātrā* = eighth note. Bārhaspatyam (GG 91.1).

Example 7 (T). 1 *mātrā* = sixteenth note. Mahāvaiśvāmitram I (GG 343.6).

Example 8 (T). 1 *mātrā* = sixteenth note. Sāṃvargaḥ (GG 11.1).

Example 9 (T). 1 *mātrā* = eighth note. Āmahīyavam (ŪG 1.1.1).

The NK Sāmavedīs are inconsistent, sometimes doubling when conjucts or differently notated syllables follow, sometimes not. Their ambivalence is reflected in this extract, where the *mātrā*'s value changes from an eighth note, as on the first syllable, to a sixteenth note on the remaining syllables with short vowels.
Example 10 (NK). 1 *mātrā* = eighth note. Gāyatram.

It is worth noting that the Kauthumas of North India (Gujarāt/Vārāṇasī) assign one *mātrā* to each syllable with a short vowel, irrespective of the presence of conjuncts (see Howard 1986 : 335).

When 1-notated short syllables are closed by *anunāsika (m̐)* both the T and NK singers extend them even beyond the value of a prolated syllable, although a tripartite division can be hypothesized.
Example 11 (T). 1 *mātrā* = eighth note. Āmahīyavam (ŪG 1.1.1).

Example 12 (NK). 1 *mātrā* = sixteenth note. Āmahīyavam (ŪG 1.1.1).

The T chanters extend the 1-notated *stobha* syllable *him* (or *hum*) to six *mātrā*s in this performance; however, the threefold division characteristic of prolated/augmented syllables is evident here as well.

Example 13 (T). 1 *mātrā* = eighth note. Gāyatram.

This *stobha* is not accorded any special treatment in Karnataka. In some manuscripts and prints this syllable is followed by the abbreviation *sthi* (for *sthiramātrā*), which indicates that a pause lasting one-half *mātrā* is to be made after *him* (see ML 2.14).

As is the case in Vārāṇasī (see Howard 1986: 337), the T singers sometimes extend the duration of short 1-notated syllables before the number sequences 2_1 *(pratyutkrama),* 1_2 *(preṅkha),* and $1SR_2$ *(vinata);* they may shorten the duration before the sequence 1_{23} *(karṣaṇa).* See the Introduction for an explanation of this type of number symbolism.

Example 14 (T). 1 *mātrā* = sixteenth note. Vāco Vratam I (ĀrG *Stobha,* before 94.1).

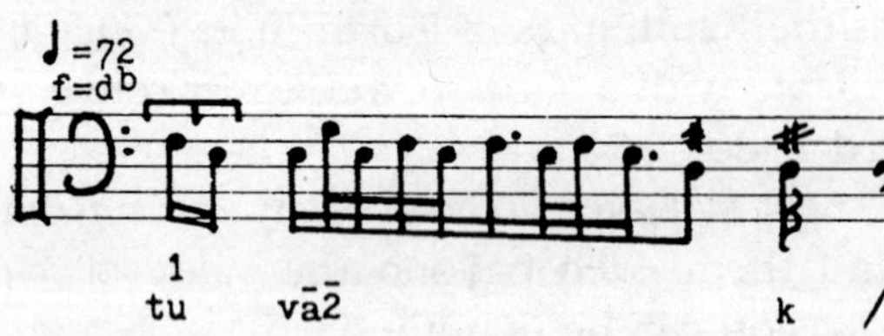

Example 15 (T). 1 *mātrā* = eighth note. Āmahīyavam (ŪG 1.1.1).

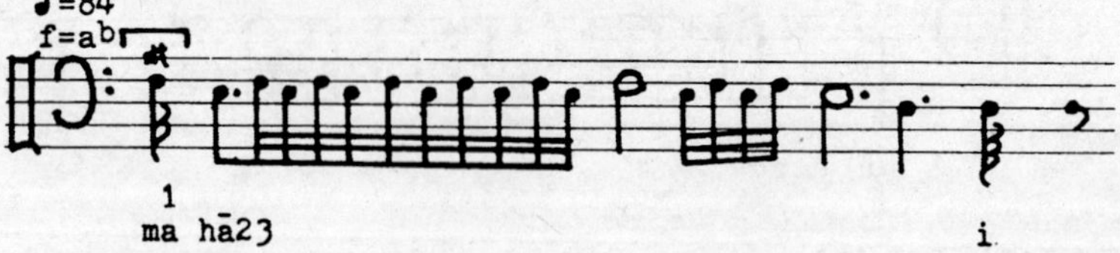

The NK Rāṇāyanīyas are inconsistent in observing this guideline.

According to NK practice, short syllables designated 2 are held far beyond their ordinary duration: ten *mātrās* resulted in the following performance, although an overall division into only three *mātrās* may be intended in theory—this is the practice in Vārāṇasī (see Howard 1986: 338).

Example 16 (NK). 1 *mātrā*=sixteenth note. Sāṃvargaḥ (GG 11.1).

Not enough specimens were provided to permit conclusions on T treatment.

B. *Long Syllables*

In the chantbooks long syllables are those with long vowels having the letter *r* placed above. Prolated and augmented syllables have long vowels that lack this notation.

1r

In both the T and NK traditions a 1r-notated syllable either final in the *parvan* or followed by a differently notated syllable often has more than four times the duration of a two-*mātrā* syllable, as this T excerpt demonstrates. The three divisions that one would expect of prolated/augmented syllables are present.

Example 17 (T). 1 *mātrā*=eighth note. Āmahīyavam (ŪG 1.1.1).

In the T style a single 1r syllable in a series of 1-notated syllables is worth two *mātrās* if it is the first syllable in the series and if prolated/augmented 1 follows at some point in the series. If it is not first in the series, it has the three divisions characteristic of prolated/augmented syllables (see Example 17).

Example 18 (T). 1 *mātrā*=sixteenth note. Hārivarṇam I (GG 383. 1).

The NK chanters may extend the duration of 1r syllables to from six to eight *mātrās* if these syllables occur in a series and are followed at some point by prolated/augmented 1. Notice, however, that the change of pitch divides each syllable into two unequal segments.

Example 19 (NK). 1 *mātrā*=eighth note. Gāyatram.

In the T tradition the second of two consecutive 1r syllables in a series of 1-notated syllables is treated as a prolated/augmented syllable, and thus is prolonged to six or more *mātrās*, but with the anticipated three divisions, if (a) it is not followed, at some point in the series, by prolated/augmented 1, or (b) the sequence *vinata* does not occur after the series. The other 1r syllable is comprised of the expected two units.

Example 20 (T). 1 *mātrā*=sixteenth note. Gautamasya Caiva Parkaḥ (GG 1.3).

Two consecutive 1r syllables in a series of 1-notated syllables are worth two or three *mātrās* each if prolated/augmented 1 follows at some point in the series or if *vinata* occurs after the series. Each syllable is comprised of two clearly defined segments, however.

Example 21 (T). 1 *mātrā*=eighth note. Kāvam (ŪG 1.1.13).

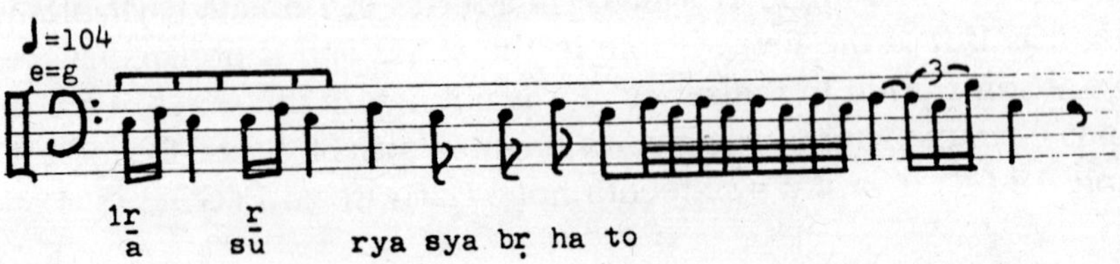

Two non-consecutive 1r syllables in a series of 1-notated syllables are comprised of two *mātrās* each.

Example 22. (T). 1 *mātrā*=sixteenth note. Rayiṣṭham (GG 512. 2).

The last of three (or more?) 1r syllables in a series of 1-notated syllables is extended to from four to six *mātrās*, with the three divisions characteristic of prolated/augmented syllables, if prolated/augmented 1 does not follow in the series (or if *vinata* does not follow the series?). The other two 1r syllables are worth two *mātrās* each.

Example 23 (T). 1 *mātrā* = sixteenth note. Kaśyapasya Barhiṣīyam (GG 1.2).

The last of three (or more?) 1r syllables in a series of 1-notated syllables does not undergo such extension if prolated/augmented 1 follows in the series (or if *vinata* occurs after the series?). It and the preceding 1r syllables are held for two *mātrās*.

Example 24 (T). 1 *mātrā* = eighth note. Gāyatram.

In the NK tradition a single 1r or the last in a series of 1r syllables is prolonged to approximately six or seven *mātrās*, with the division reminiscent of prolated/augmented syllables, if augmented 1 does not follow in the series. The other 1r syllables are comprised of three or four *mātrās*, although the change of pitch gives the impression of two *mātrās*.

Example 25 (NK). 1 *mātrā* = sixteenth note. Kaśyapasya Barhiṣīyam. (GG 1.2).

2r

An isolated 2r syllable, or the final 2r in a series of 2-notated syllables, is prolonged to varying durations, but the average length in the T style appears to be six to eight *mātrās*. A tripartite arrangement is evident, however.

Example 26 (T). 1 mātrā = eighth note. Bārhaspatyam (GG 91.1).

A 2r syllable in this same context was awarded twenty-six *mātrās* by a NK singer, but the three divisions typical of prolated/augmented syllables are present.

Example 27 (NK). 1 *mātrā* = sixteenth note. Raudram II (GG 115.3).

In a series of 2-notated syllables with several 2r syllables, all except the last consist of two *mātrās* according to this T reading.

Example 28 (T). 1 *mātrā* = sixteenth note. Gautamasya Parkaḥ (GG 1.1).

The NK Sāmavedīs observe this rule only if two or four or more 2r syllables occur in the series. If three occur, then only the second of two consecutive 2r syllables is worth two *mātrās*.

Example 29 (NK). 1 *mātrā* = eighth note. Rathantaram (ŪhyG 1.1.1).

However, three or more 2r syllables prior to a final 2r consist of one or two *mātrās* in this NK interpretation. Note that the two pitches associated with each syllable produce two clearly defined divisions.

Example 30 (NK). 1 *mātrā* = eighth note. Bhakāra-Rathantaram (on ŪhyG 1.1.1).

3r

According to this T reading, a 3r-notated syllable prior to a differently notated syllable is worth five *mātrās*. Two overall divisions are heard, however.

Example 31 (T). 1 *mātrā*=eighth note. Vāmadevyam (ŪG 1.1.5).

The NK singers may allot as much as sixteen *mātrās* to such a syllable, although here a tripartite structure can be visualized.

Example 32 (NK). 1 *mātrā*=sixteenth note. Vāmadevyam (ŪG 1.1.5).

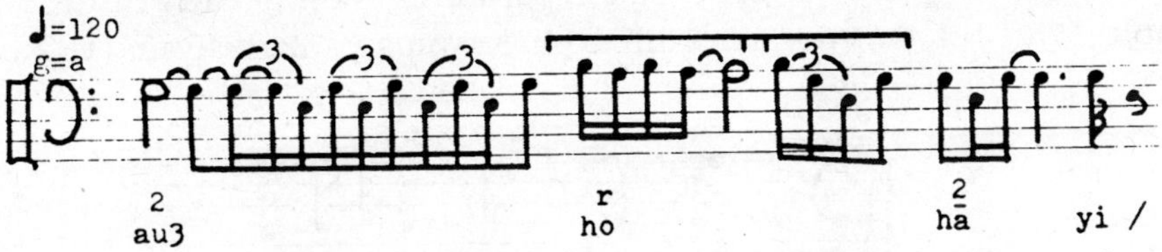

However, when 3r is followed by the sequence 2 ₃ the NK chanters reduce the duration (to six *mātrās* here, arranged in two segments).

Example 33 (NK). 1 *mātrā*=sixteenth note. Raudram I (GG 115.2).

4r

Initial 4r before 5 embraces seven *mātrās*, distributed over three sections, in this T realization (details on NK practice are not available).

Example 34 (T). 1 *mātrā*=eighth note. Bārhaspatyam (GG 91.1).

But initial 4r before the sequence 5_6 contains about two *mātrās* in this passage.

Example 35 (T). 1 *mātrā* = eighth note. Rathantaram (ŪhyG 1.1.1).

The NK chanters render the identical excerpt in four *mātrās*, but segmentation into two equal parts is possible.

Example 36 (NK). 1 *mātrā* = sixteenth note. Rathantaram (ŪhyG 1.1.1).

A 4r syllable between two 5-notated syllables contains six or seven *mātrās* in each tradition. There seems to be a bipartite division in each case.

Example 37 (T). 1 *mātrā* = sixteenth note. Kaśyapasya Barhiṣīyam (GG 1.2).

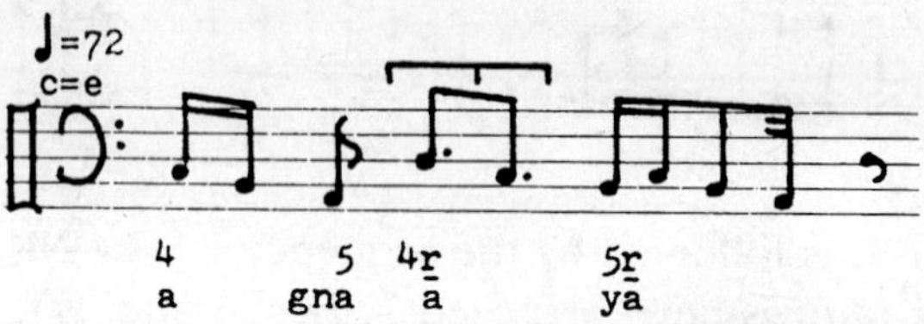

Example 38 (NK). 1 *mātrā* = sixteenth note. Kaśyapasya Barhiṣīyam (GG 1.2).

When 4r is preceded by the sequence 2_3 (or by a 3- or 4-notated syllable), then this 4r has two or three *mātrās* in the T tradition, four to fourteen *mātrās* in that of NK. In both cases a division into two segments can be postulated.

Example 39 (T). 1 *mātrā* = eighth note. Āmahīyavam (ŪG 1.1.1).

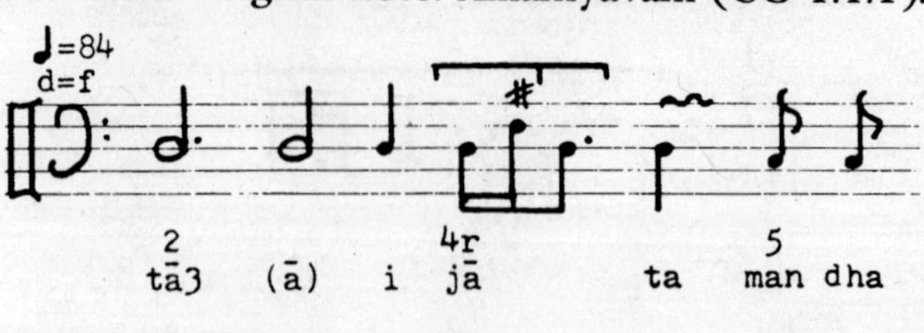

Example 40 (NK). 1 *mātrā*=sixteenth note. Āmahīyavam (ŪG 1.1.1).

A 4r syllable final in the *parvan* and occurring after the sequence 1_{234} is allotted five or six *mātrās* in T, twenty or more *mātrās* in NK. The proper segmentation into larger divisions is not readily apparent : a two- or three-part scheme is possible in each case.

Example 41 (T). 1 *mātrā*=eighth note. Rathantaram (ŪhyG 1.1.1).

Example 42 (NK). 1 *mātrā*=sixteenth note. Rathantaram (ĀrG 49.1).

5r

According to the T practice, in a series of 5-notated syllables the first of two consecutive 5r syllables comprises two *mātrās*, provided that another 5r does not appear in the series. The second 5r syllable in this context contains six or seven *mātrās*, distributed over three segments.

Example 43 (T). 1 *mātrā*=sixteenth note. Gautamasya Parkaḥ (GG 1.1).

Example 44 (T). 1 *mātrā*=sixteenth note. Rayiṣṭham (GG 512.2).

The NK chanters assign about four *mātrās* to the first 5r, as much as twenty-two *mātrās* to the second. Two and three divisions, respectively, result.
Example 45 (NK). 1 *mātrā* = sixteenth note. Mārgīyavam (GG 115.1).

Example 46 (NK). 1 *mātrā* = sixteenth note. Raudram I (GG 115.2).

However, in this tradition when two consecutive 5r syllables are followed at some point by a third 5r, the first has about fourteen *mātrās* allotted to three sections, the second six *mātrās* allotted to two sections, the third in excess of twenty *mātrās* allotted to three sections.
Example 47 (NK). 1 *mātrā* = sixteenth note. Raudram II (GG 115.3).

A single 5r syllable, including those followed by differently notated syllables and those final in the *parvan,* is worth approximately six *mātrās* in T, slightly more or less in NK. The proper segmentation is not readily apparent, but a two- rather than a three-part arrangement seems to be more plausible.
Example 48 (T). 1 *mātrā* = sixteenth note. Sāṃvargaḥ (GG 11.1).

Example 49 (T). 1 *mātrā*=sixteenth note. Rayiṣṭham (GG 512.2).

Example 50 (NK). 1 *mātrā*=sixteenth note. Āmahīyavam (ŪG 1.1.1).

Example 51 (NK). 1 *mātrā*=sixteenth note. Indrasya Priyam II (GG 372.2).

C. *Prolated/Augmented Syllables*

Prolated/Augmented 1

In the T tradition prolated/augmented 1 may possess ten times the value of a short syllable. Three overall divisions are discernible, however.
Example 52 (T). 1 *mātrā* = eighth note. Gāyatram.

However, when two prolated/augmented 1 syllables occur in succession, the first is abbreviated (usually five to seven *mātrās*). This abbreviation may take place also when short 1 follows. In such cases two instead of three divisions result.
Example 53 (T). 1 *mātrā* = eighth note. Rathantaram (ŪhyG 1.1.1).

An ensuing sequence beginning with figure 1 (1234, for instance) may also cause shortening of a preceding prolated/augmented 1 syllable. The NK chanters likewise extend prolated/augmented 1 far beyond the bounds of three *mātrās.* In the following example it consists of nearly two dozen *mātrās*, although a tripartite arrangement may be intended.
Example 54 (NK). 1 *mātrā* = sixteenth note. Mārgīyavam (GG 115.1).

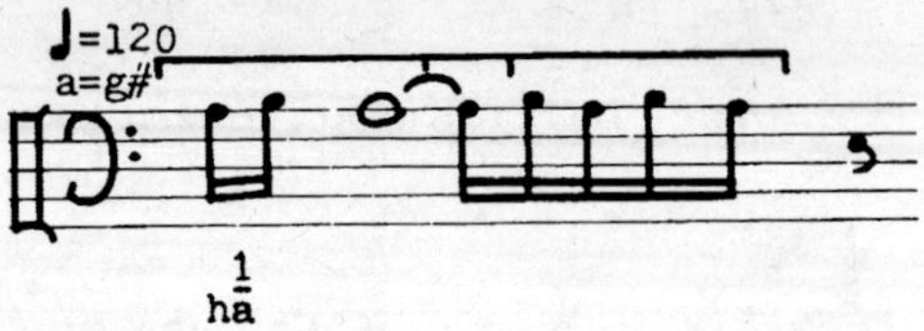

However, they also abbreviate under the conditions just described (to four *mātrās* in this excerpt). Two segments result here as well.
Example 55 (NK). 1 *mātrā* = eighth note. Gāyatraṃ.

In a series of 1-notated syllables with two or more non-consecutive prolated/augmented syllables, they sing all but the last of these as ordinary 1r syllables (three *mātrās* in this instance, although the two tones give an impression of a bipartite division).
Example 56 (NK). 1 *mātrā* = eighth note. Gāyatram.

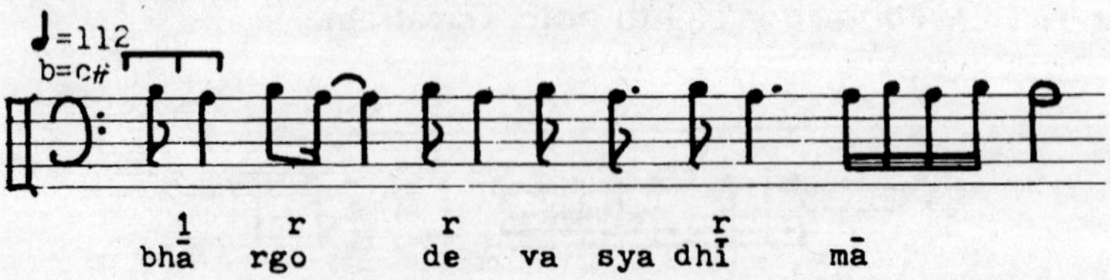

Prolated/Augmented 2

In both traditions prolated/augmented 2 is normally held six to ten times the duration of a short vowel. A three-part division is probably understood to be present but will not be specified in the following two examples.
Example 57 (T). 1 *mātrā* = eighth note. Vāmadevyam (ŪG 1.1.5).

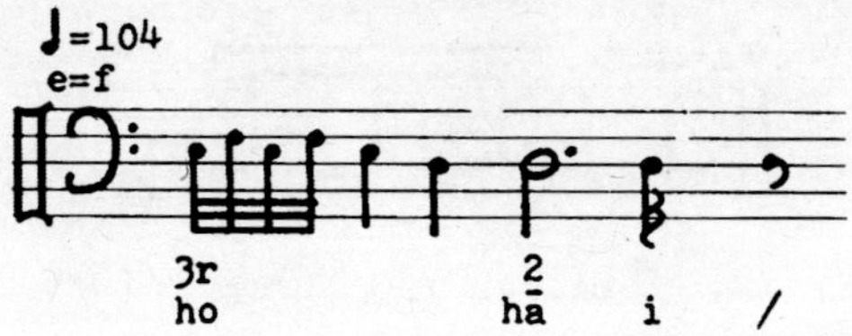

Example 58 (NK). 1 *mātrā* = sixteenth note. Vāmadevyam (ŪG 1.1.5).

Prolated/Augmented 3

(Examples of prolated/augmented 3 are absent in the transcribed specimens.)

Prolated/Augmented 4

In the following two examples initial prolated/augmented 4 followed by prolated/augmented 4 that is final in the *parvan* lasts nine *mātrā*s in the T interpretation, about five *mātrā*s according to NK practice. An overall triple division is suggested.

Example 59 (T). 1 *mātrā* = sixteenth note. Gautamasya Parkaḥ (GG 1.1).

Example 60 (NK). 1 *mātrā* = sixteenth note. Gautamasya Parkaḥ (GG 1.1).

Final prolated/augmented 4 is allotted from five to eight *mātrā*s in T, from two to seven *mātrā*s in NK (where the duration depends on the pitch of the preceding tone). Ordinarily the effect is that of division into three segments.

Example 61 (T). 1 *mātrā* = sixteenth note. Kaśyapasya Barhiṣīyam (GG 1.2).

Example 62 (NK). 1 *mātrā* = sixteenth note. Kaśyapasya Barhiṣīyam (GG 1.2).

Example 63 (NK). 1 *mātrā* = sixteenth note. Gautamasya Caiva Parkaḥ (GG 1.3).

Example 64 (NK). 1 *mātrā* = sixteenth note. Gautamasya Parkaḥ (GG 1.1).

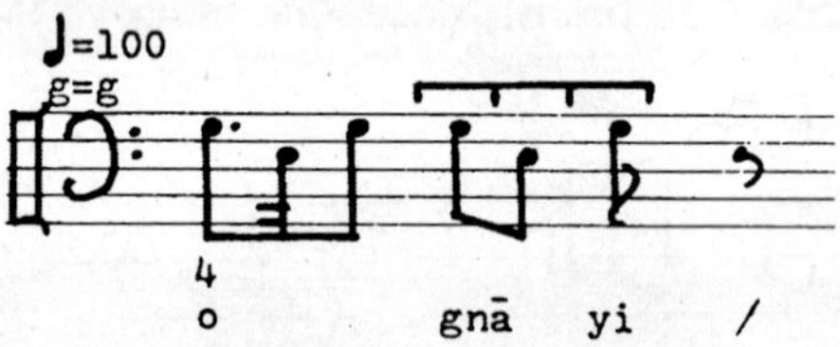

Initial or medial prolated/augmented 4 before and/or following a 5-notated syllable is worth about five to eight *mātrās*, grouped apparently into two sections, in T, approximately twelve *mātrās*, grouped possibly into three sections, in NK. Example 65 (T). 1 *mātrā* = sixteenth note. Mahāvaiśvāmitram I (GG 343.6).

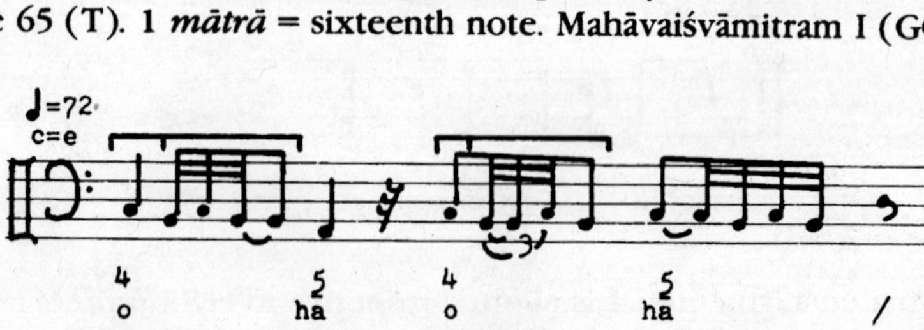

Example 66 (NK). 1 *mātrā* = sixteenth note. Mārgīyavam (GG 115.1).

Medial prolated/augmented 4 preceded by a 3- or 4-notated syllable and followed by a (final?) 5-notated syllable contains approximately three *mātrā*s, sometimes more, according to T realization.

Example 67 (T). 1 *mātrā* = sixteenth note. Janitram II (GG 484.2).

The NK habit is to assign about six *mātrā*s to this type of syllable. Whether a duple or triple division is intended is open to question.

Example 68 (NK). 1 *mātrā* = sixteenth note. Vāmadevyam (ŪG 1.1.5).

However, when prolated/augmented 4 immediately precedes, this syllable's duration is increased to eleven *mātrā*s, grouped in three sections; the preceding syllable possesses two *mātrā*s.

Example 69 (NK). 1 *mātrā* = sixteenth note. Indrasya Priyam III (GG 372.2).

Prolated/Augmented 5

In T initial prolated/augmented 5 followed by final prolated/augmented 5 contains five or six *mātrā*s (three overall divisions). An NK Brāhmaṇ gave only two *mātrā*s to the identical syllable.

Example 70 (T). 1 *mātrā* = eighth note. Rathantaram (ŪhyG 1.1.1).

Example 71 (NK). 1 *mātrā* = eighth note. Rathantaram (ŪhyG 1.1.1).

Medial prolated/augmented 5 is worth three or four *mātrās* in each tradition. A bipartite division is obvious in each instance.

Example 72 (T). 1 *mātrā* = sixteenth note. Mahāvaiśvāmitram I (GG 343.6).

Example 73 (NK). 1 *mātrā* = sixteenth note. Kaśyapasya Barhiṣīyam (GG 1.2).

In the T and NK traditions final prolated/augmented 5 is comprised of approximately three to seven *mātrāa*, grouped into three divisions, if the syllable is without *gati* elongation (see ML 1.15, 3.1-2) or is not closed by a consonant (excluding nasals) or *visarga (ḥ). Parvans* consisting solely of single prolated/augmented 5 also have this value.

Example 74 (T). 1 *mātrā* = eighth note. Vāmadevyam (ŪG 1.1.5).

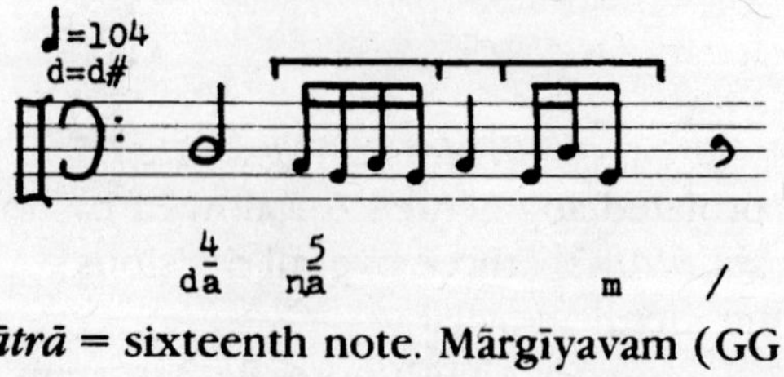

Example 75 (NK). 1 *mātrā* = sixteenth note. Mārgīyavam (GG 115.1).

Final prolated/augmented 5 extended by the addition of *gati* or possessing a final consonant (including *visarga*) is worth from three to five *mātrās* in T, around fifteen *mātrās* in NK. Presumably, under these conditions *parvans* consisting solely of a single prolated/augmented 5 syllable also have this duration. A threefold division is manifested in both traditions.

Example 76 (T). 1 *mātrā* = eighth note. Vāmadevyam (ŪG 1.1.5).

Example 77 (NK). 1 *mātrā* = sixteenth note. Mārgīvavam (GG 115.1)

4

In Sharma 1969 : 25 it is pointed out "[these] sentences [of the commentary] are vague" and that "it is clear that many words, perhaps even passages, have been left out here by the scribe." Verse 555 of the Pūrvārcika ends with the word *dhiyaḥ,* which, in the two Sāmarājam chants (GG 555. 4-5), becomes

3 5
dhī234yāḥ
and
4
dhā5yā656ḥ,
respectively. In both cases prolation is present on the final vowel, although the second example is extended from three to twelve *mātrās* through the addition of the figures 6, 5, and 6—each worth three *mātrās* (see the notes to ML 1.19).

5

The sacred syllable *ōm* is found at the end of the *prastāva* section of the Gāyatram *("tat savitur vareṇiyŌM," "upāsmai gayatā narŌM,"* and so forth)

and at the beginning of the *udgītha* section. During the Vedic ritual the Udgātr priest replaces the original syllables of the *udgītha-* and *upadrava-*sections of the Gāyatram by *ō*-vowels, representing *ōm*. However, the three and one-half measurement does not apply to these *ōkāras*, which possess the durations of the original syllables (see Howard 1983: 323-24). It is the practice of some chanters to preface each and every chant with the sacred syllable. The *ōm* that introduces the *udgītha* has very near the measurement prescribed by the ML (see Howard 1983: 323), if *mātrā* is to be interpreted strictly as the length of a short syllable. However, the *ōm* that concludes the *prastāva* consists of approximately three overall segments (see Example 52). Presumably the extra one-half *mātrā* belongs to the final *m* (see the commentary on ML 1.6).

6

In the Sāmavedic chants those syllables having short vowels, and consequently the one-*mātrā* time value, ordinarily are heard for only a fraction of a second and hence are musically rather unimportant. The duration of these short vowels is not the same as that of individual consonants, which possess one-half *mātrā*. It is noted in Allen 1953: 84 that "the *mātrā* concept has no justification in connexion with consonants," despite statements to the contrary in the Taittirīya-and Vājasaneyi-Prātiśākhyas. Assignment of time value of consonants is, therefore, nothing more than a theoretical exercise.

7

The traditional order of the simple vowels is *a, ā, i, ī, u, ū, ṛ, ṝ*. Each short vowel and the long vowel that follows it belong to a specific phonetic class. Vowels *a,* and *ā* are "glottal" sounds in that they are produced at the glottis, the opening between the vocal cords in the larynx. Vowels *i* and *ī* are described as "palatal" because they originate with the middle of the tongue raised near the palate, the roof of the mouth. Vowels *u* and *ū* are "labial" sounds due to the roundness and protrusion of the lips when these vowels are articulated. Vowels *ṛ* and *ṝ* are "retroflex", that is, sounded by raising and bending backwards the tip of the tongue.

8

The diphthongs are the vowels *e, o, ai,* and *au*. They are composites of simple vowels: *e* = *a* + *i*, *o* = *a* + *u*, *ai* = *ā* + *i*, *au* = *ā* + *u*. When it is considered that *ā* = *a* + *a*, the commentator's statement that the diphthongs owe their existence to the prefixed *a*-vowel becomes understandable. They are classified according to the quality of the second of the two vowels. Hence *e* and *ai* are viewed as palatal, *o* and *au* as labial.

10

Vowels are the carriers of musical sound and are named *svaras* as a result. This holds true for recited verses as well as for chanted melodies. The quotation in the commentary is a play on the term *svara* ("sound"). The reader is reminded that the Vedic *svara* is not the same as the *svara* of the classical music, where the term refers to a degree of a scale.

11

The time value of the *kalā* is absolute, while the *mātrā's* duration depends on the tempo selected by the chanter. According to Nārada-Śikṣā 1.6.21, "one should perform in the fast *vṛtti* (style) when studying, but in a moderate tempo when reciting, and in the slow *vṛtti* for the instruction of pupils" (Rowell 1977 : 89).

Kalā is a Vedic word that appears, for instance, in the Ṛgveda, the Taittirīya-Saṃhitā, the Śatapatha-Brāhmaṇa, and the Ṣaḍviṃśa-Brāhmaṇa. *Kalā* is perhaps derived from the root *kal* ("to calculate, to enumerate"), as is the similar word *Kāla* ("time"). In its Vedic sense *kalā* implies "a part of something." Its use in designating a subdivision of the *mātrā* is met not only in the ML but also in Dvijarājabhaṭṭa's commentary on Saṃhitopaniṣad-Brāhmaṇa 1.21, where he quotes ML 1.11-12 and Nārada-Śikṣā 1.6.21 (see Sharma 1965 30-31). The *brāhmaṇa* passage refers to the three tempi not as fast *(druta)*, moderate *(madhyama)*, and slow *(vilambita)* but as entirely unaugmented *(sarvāvṛddha)*, entirely augmented *(sarvavṛddha)*, and additionally augmented and [sung] in secret *(utsedhaparokṣavṛddha)*. In his commentary Dvijarājabhaṭṭa echoes the declaration in the ML (which he calls Chandogapariśiṣṭa) that the fast tempo *(avṛddha)* contains 3 *kalās*, the moderate *(vṛddha)* 4, the slow *(utsedhaparokṣavṛddha)* 5. However, he emphasizes that these tempi are related by the *brāhmaṇa* to the *ārcika*, the collection of source verses. Hence the 3 : 4 : 5 correspondence holds true for recited verses as well as for chanted melodies. In the introduction to Sharma 1965 : 30-31 it is stated that Dvijarājabhaṭṭa may have lived in the fifteenth century. If this is so, then the ML, which he quotes, must be at least that old. He does not refer to the ML author(s) by name but calls him/them instead the *"pariśiṣṭakāras."* Concerning the age of the Saṃhitopaniṣad-Brāhmaṇa, Parpola has given reasons for supposing that it is a very ancient work predating the Lāṭyāyana-Śrautasūtra, which he estimates was composed between 400 and 300 B.C. (see Parpola 1968 : 28, 89; Parpola 1969 : 242-243, n. 2). If this is true, then the characterization of the tempi as *sarvāvṛddha*, and so on, may be the original one.

12

The colours assigned to the three tempi are also those associated with Vāyu, whose chariot is pulled by red horses, with Bṛhaspati, who has a blue back, and with Sūrya, who is called a white and brilliant horse (see Macdonell 1898 : 82,

101, 31). Saṃhitopaniṣad-Brāhmaṇa 1.21 (see above) connects the three tempi to Vāyu, Indra, and Agni.

13

The meaning appears to be that one tempo must be kept throughout. Tempo cannot be changed from one syllable to the next; therefore, in the course of a chant the *mātrā* has a fixed value.

15

Gati ("[vocalic] affix") involves the addition of *i* or *u* to *ā* and the resulting formation of a diphthong from a simple vowel. However, there are instances of *gati* appendages to diphthongs; moreover, the semivowel *y* may be inserted between the two vowels (*hoyi* is an example of both of these practices). Whereas normal diphthongal pronunciation requires the rather rapid coalescence of the two sounds, in the Sāmavedic chants the first vowel is held for a discernible period of time, after which the second vowel is intoned fairly quickly. Therefore, there is a clear distinction between the two vowels—in fact, in the chants the vowels are written separately (*āi* in place of the customary *ai*, *āu* instead of *au*) and have specific time values allotted to them (see ML 3.2). Yet, even with the interpolated *y*, the two letters are considered components of a single syllable, which may be either long or augmented. Why did the composers of the chants utilize this method of vowel modification? It would appear that there was a vocal preference for the glottal vowel *ā*, especially on syllables that were musically prolonged.

16

Having discussed the short, long, and prolated/augmented classifications of those syllables with only a single notated numeral, the ML author now proceeds to give the durations of syllables having two or more figures. Those numbers after the first are given not above but within the textual line, after the syllable in question. Prolated/augmented syllables and syllables with sequences carry the principal musical phrases in a given chant. A syllable with a sequence is classified by the ML according to whether it does or does not have the time value of syllables in the *ārcika*, the collection of accented source verses. As a rule, in the *ārcika* syllables are either short or long (one or two *mātrās*). The "syllable divorced from accentuation" (*visvaram akṣaram*) has a value in excess of that allowed on *ārcika* syllables, for each notated numeral is worth three *mātrās*. Those sequences having the time value of *ārcika* syllables (*ārciko 'kṣarakālaḥ*) are discussed elsewhere (ML 3.3-7).

17

Those sequences with durations above those of the accented source verses are given the names *pratyutkrama* ("ascent" : see Simon 1908 : 521, Simon 1913 : 313-14, Howard 1977 : 44-48), *atikrama* ("omission" : see Simon 1908 : 516, Simon 1913 : 313, Howard 1977 : 48-50), *karṣaṇa* ("extension" : see Simon

1908 : 518-20, Simon 1913 : 314, Howard 1977 : 50-62), and *svāra* ("having [musical] sound" : see Simon 1908: 525, Simon 1913, 315, Howard 1977: 66-69).

19

The second sentence of the commentary is partially corrupt (see Sharma 1969 : 147). Of the two quotations from the *gānas*, the following occurs in several *sāmans*, including the chant that is specified :

5
vā656 (GG 396. 1 : Śundhyus Sāma).

The fragment *vāyuḥ javāno ho* has not been identified. The second quotation refers to

3 2 4
kay ā3sthā5irā656n (GG 13. 1 : Śnābham).

The sequence 5_{656} is termed *parisvāra.* It has the *pratyutkrama* feature in that ascent is made from the *atisvārya mudrā* (the lower end of the little finger) to the low *mudrā* (the middle of the little finger). Since this sequence contains four numerals, each worth three *mātrās*, a total of twelve *mātrās* results. A T Sāmavedī exceeds this duration by seven *mātrās;* if one were to divide the music into twelve approximately equal segments, each segment would be roughly equivalent to a quarter note, not an eighth note. Rather than specifying the sequence as

5
ṇā656 . . . ḥ,

I have spaced out the four numbers in order to indicate the probable spots where the corresponding *mātrās* occur. In other examples as well I have adapted the numbers of a sequence to the music that they symbolize.

Example 78 (T). 1 *mātrā* = eighth note. Kāvam (ŪG 1.1.13).

As far as the total number of *mātrās* is concerned, the NK chanters come very close to the prescription of the ML (see Howard 1977 : 130). However, the apportionment of *mātrā* among the numerals is uneven and hence will not be indicated. With each appearance of numeral 6 they nasalize, thus giving credence to an optional name for the sequence : *padānusvāra* (see Simon 1908 : 521, Howard 1977 : 45).

Example 79 (NK). 1 *mātrā* = sixteenth note. Tānvam II (GG 128.2) and Syaumaraśmam II (GG 323.4).

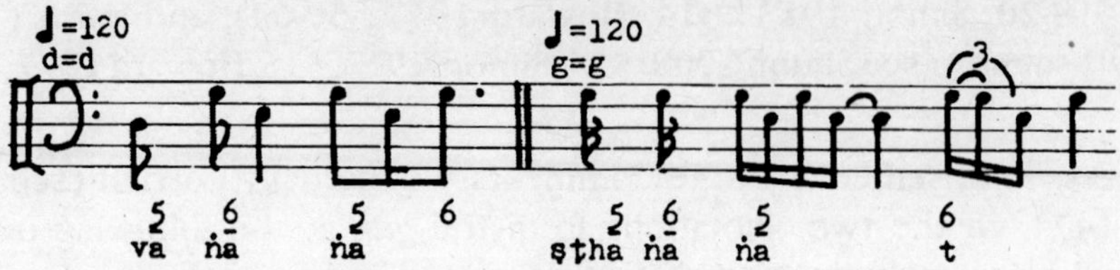

Like the T Sāmavedīs, the Jaiminīyas do not nasalize at the places where 5_{656} is found in the notation. Their syllable notation has the conjunct *tr* as the 5_{656} equivalent (see Howard 1988).

20

Examples of 5_4 have not been transcribed. The sequence should bear two + three = five *mātrā*s (see ML 2.3).

21

According to the T practice the sequence 4_3 consists of the ML-prescribed six *mātrā*s only when followed by 2r (or short or prolated/augmented 2?), in which case it should contain not six but five *mātrā*s (see ML 2.3). When followed by 2_3 or when final in the *parvan,* 4_3 exceeds this valuation. Dividing the music into five or six segments would be speculative.

Example 80 (T). 1 *mātrā* = sixteenth note in the first extract, an eighth note in the remaining specimens. Vāco Vratam II (ĀrG *stobha,* before 94.1), Vāmadevyam (ŪG 1.1.5), Rathantaram (ŪhyG 1.1.1), Rathantaram (ŪhyG 1.1.1).

The NK singers always assign more time units to 4_3 than the ML allows : three or four times the expected duration is common, although six uneven segments are perceivable in this example (where 4_3 is final in the *parvan*).

Example 81 (NK). 1 *mātrā* = sixteenth note. Rathantaram (ĀrG 49.1).

The Jaiminīya symbol corresponding to 4_3 is the compound sign *ṇ-ph* (see Howard 1988).

22

According to ML 2.3 the first two numbers of the pattern 3_{234} should have five *mātrās* not six : two units should be allotted to 3, three units to 2. Hence eleven *mātrās* should result from the four *mudrās*. In fact, eleven unequal segments can be postulated in the following T excerpt.

Example 82 (T). 1 *mātrā* = eighth note. Bārhaspatyam (GG 91.1).

Although they tend to exceed the expected durations, the NK Sāmavedīs give more emphasis to 3 than to 2. Postulating eleven divisions would amount to sheer speculation.

Example 83 (NK). 1 *mātrā* = sixteenth note. Gautamasya Parkaḥ (GG 1.1) and Mārgīyavam (GG 115.1).

The Jaiminīya equivalent of 3_{234} —and also, in fact, of 3_{2345}^{111}—is ***kh*** (see Howard 1988).

23

The *pratyutkrama pattern* 2_1 should likewise consist of five *mātrās* (see ML 2.3). The following extract from a T performance gives four *mātrās* to the second *mudrā*, about five *mātrās* to the first. However, five segments, each a quarter-note in duration, are apparent in the example.

Example 84 (T). 1 *mātrā* = eighth note. Āmahīyavam (ŪG 1.1.1).

When realized by a NK chanter the two numbers possess six and seven *mātrās*, respectively. Here too a quintuple division, though one consisting of unequal segments, has been devised.

Example 85 (NK). 1 *mātrā* = sixteenth note. Gautamasya Caiva Parkaḥ (GG 1.3).

The sequence has *y* as its counterpart in the Jaiminīya syllablic system (see Parpola 1973 : 19, 21; Howard 1988).

24

The syllable *pā* or the word ^{0}*pāvne* is divided between two successive *parvans*:

5r 3r
. . . pā / ā . . . .

Therefore, in this unusual case a sequence is not involved; the two components combined amount to four *mātrā*s (see ML 2.6). This chant was not recorded by me.

25

A rare occurrence of 5_2, as interpreted by a NK Brāhmaṇ, shows twelve *mātrā*s on the low (fifth) *mudrā*, sixteen on the second. Theoretically the sequence should possess three + three = six *mātrās*; however, a two + three segmentation is apparent here.

Example 86 (NK). 1 *mātrā* = sixteenth note. Aidaṃ Kāvam (GG 554.2).

26

Pratyutkrama from 3 to 1 occurs, for example, between the final two numbers of the sequence 2_{31}. A T singer gave two *mātrās* to the third *mudrā*, five to the first. Here the sequence 2_3 (*praṇata*: see ML 3.3-5), worth two *mātrās*, is extended by means of a three-*mātrā mudrā*. Five unequal divisions are apparent here.

Example 87 (T). 1 *mātrā* = sixteenth note. Yaśaḥ Sāma (ĀrG 61.1).

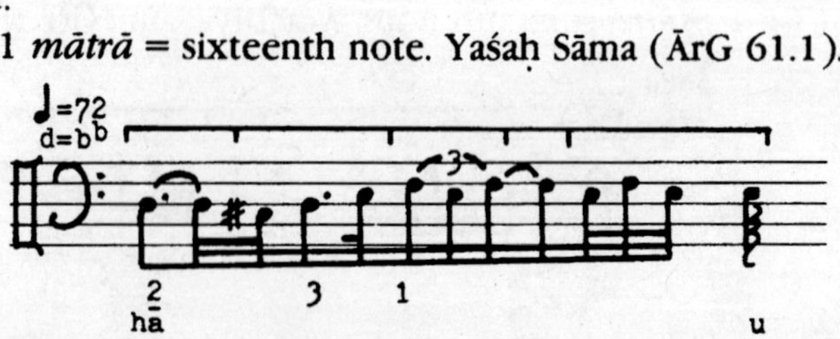

In a NK reading 3 has three or four *mātrās*, while 1 possesses ten *mātrās*. A five-part segmentation is heard here as well.

Example 88 (NK). 1 *mātrā* = sixteenth note. Śaikhaṇḍinam I (GG 342.1).

(GG 342.1).

NK executions of 2_{312} and 2_{31234}, both extensions of *praṇata*, likewise show about three *mātrās* for the third *mudrā*; however, the *svara* connected with the thumb is held up to nineteen *mātrās*. The first three numbers of each sequence would be divisible into five parts, as in the previous example.

Example 89 (NK). 1 *mātrā* = sixteenth note. Vāravantīyam II (GG 17.2).

Example 90 (NK). 1 *mātrā* = sixteenth note. Ṛtusāma II (GG 64.2).

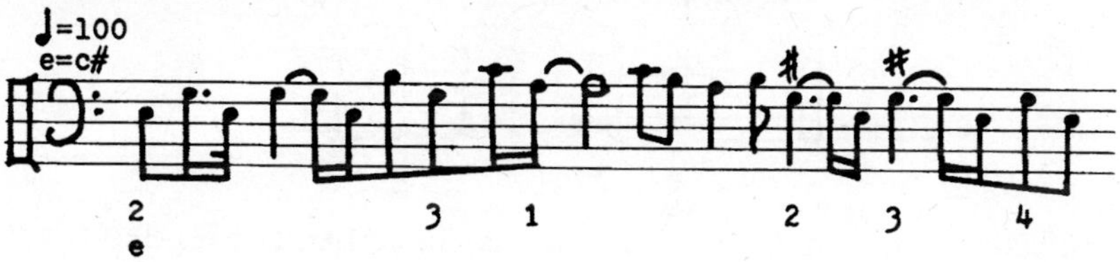

27

Atikrama involves the omission of one or more fingers in skipping from one *mudrā* to another. This omission may take place either in ascent or descent, although the ascending patterns (5 to 3, 5 to 2, and 3 to 1) have already been discussed as examples of *pratyutkrama* (see also Howard 1977: 46, 49-50). Therefore, only the four descending types are identified here. The commentator saves his remarks until the conclusion of the *atikrama* precepts.

28, 29, 30, 31.

Ordinarily the symbol 11 is used to designate *kruṣṭa* in the chantbooks (see Howard 1977: 30-31). In South India, and occasionally in the North, the *kruṣṭa-mudrā* is kept distinct from the *prathama-mudrā* (see Howard 1977: 105-8): accordingly, the thumb is held at a distance of one *yava* (the length of a barley corn) above the index finger when the *prathama-mudrā* is desired, two *yavas* above when the *kruṣṭa-mudrā* is called for (see Tarlekar 1985:69) This hand position may well be a later addition to the notation, for Puṣpasūtra 9.26 declares that the *kruṣṭa-svar* occurs in only two chants (see Simon 1908: 712; Howard 1977:30, n. 2; Tarlekar 1985:73). The peculiar method of effecting *atikrama* of 1 in crossing from 11 to 2 has already been illustrated, in Howard

1977: 105-6. Here a T interpretation shows sixteen *mātrā*s connected with the *kruṣṭa-mudrā*, only one or two *mātrā*s with the second *mudrā*. The habit of the NK Brāhmaṇs in this matter has not been documented.

Atikrama of 2 in crossing from 1 to 3 is known also as *namana* (see Howard 1977: 62-64: in Tarlekar 1985:58 *namana* is identified as 1_32). It is customary to place the *avagraha* (ऽ) above the syllable bearing the sequence. In a T performance six *mātrās* are given to the first *mudrā*, only two *mātrā*s to the third. The overall division shows three segments connected with 1, only one segment with 3.

Example 91 (T). 1 *mātrā*=sixteenth note. Rayiṣṭham (GG 512.2).

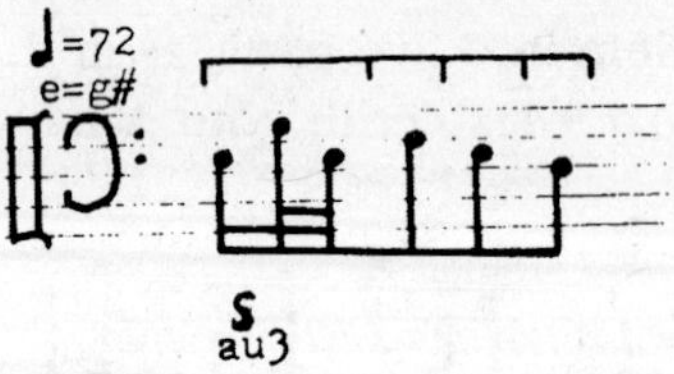

A NK Brāhamaṇ assigns twelve *mātrā*s to 1, four *mātrā*s to 3. Five divisions are in evidence here (3 is followed by 2_3).

Example 92 (NK). 1 *mātrā*=sixteenth note. Indrasya Priyam II (GG 372.2).

One comes across instances of *namana* that have been extended through the addition of extra numbers. Such an example is the following specimen, where a T Brāhmaṇ gives the three numbers seven, two, and one *mātrā*s, respectively. The melodic contour suggests an apportionment that assigns only one division to numbers 3 and 2.

Example 93 (T). 1 *mātrā*=eighth note. Bārhaspatyam (GG 91.1).

The identical sequence has sixteen, seven, and two *mātrā*s assigned to the respective numbers according to a NK reading. Here 3 is apportioned into the expected two sections (see ML 2.3).

Example 94 (NK). 1 *mātrā*=sixteenth note. Āśvam (GG 116.1).

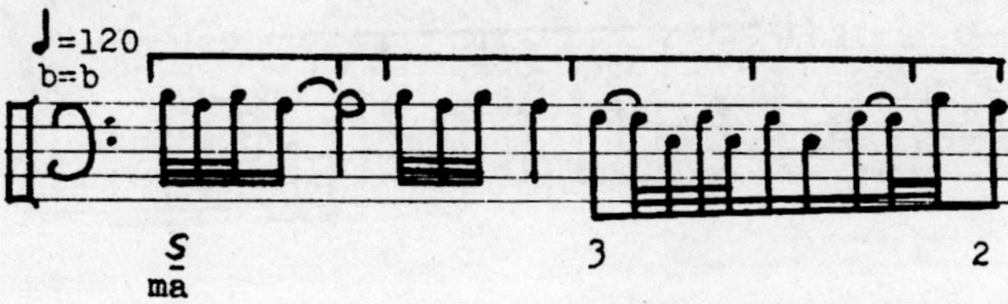

Sometimes the degree of extension reaches snakelike proportions, as in this NK excerpt. The length of the sequence has resulted in melodic compression; hence the overall divisions are obscured.

Example 95 (NK). 1 *mātrā*=sixteenth note. Vāmram Praiyamedham Vā III (GG 166.3).

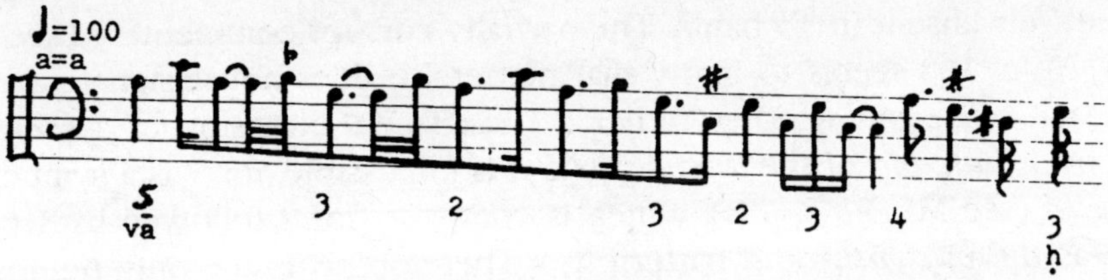

Atikrama of 4 in crossing from 3 to 5 comes close to having the expected six *mātrā*s in this T interpretation. However, the overall segmentation appears to be along the lines three+two.

Example 96 (T). 1 *mātrā*=eighth note. Vāmadevyam (ŪG 1.1.5).

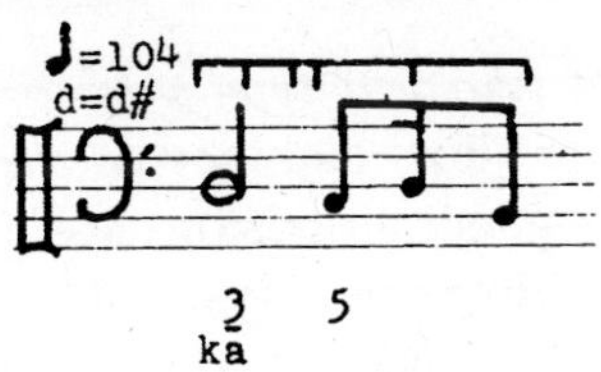

A NK version gives the two numbers sixteen *mātrā*s, but here also a fivefold division can be hypothesized.

Example 97 (NK). 1 *mātrā*=sixteenth note. Vāmadevyam (ŪG 1.1.5).

This type of *atikrama* is one of several numbers or number combinations connected with the Jaiminīya symbol *ph* (see Howard 1988).

Atikrama of 2, 3, and 4 in crossing from 1 to 5 is available only in a NK reading, where approximately twenty *mātrā*s are involved. The six anticipated divisions are present.

Example 98 (NK). 1 *mātrā*=sixteenth note. Aśvinor Vratam I (ĀrG 103.1).

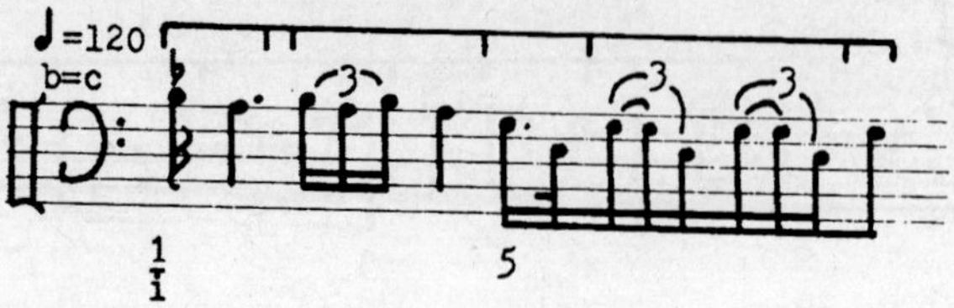

32.

The five types of *karṣaṇa* ("extension") are 1_2, 1_{23}, 1_{234}, 1_{2345}, and 5_6. The first is known as *preṅkha* ("shaking": see Burnell 1876:xlii, Howard 1977: 64-66), a term that has been in vogue more recently. The pattern 5_6 is another type of *parisvāra* or *padānusvāra* (see ML 1.19) in that nasalization of the vowel preceding the 6-notation is required. This is apparent in the NK tradition but entirely absent in T chants. The partially corrupt commentary (see Sharma 1969:13, n. 16) seems to imply that numeral 6 does not designate a *svara* in the usual sense but denotes rather a (nasalized) extension of a *svara* on 5. Moreover, *karṣaṇa* of the *atisvārya* (6_7) is impossible, for 7 is a symbol of the *abhigīta* (see ML 3.3-4, 7-8), which is comprised of 2 followed by 1 (not the same as the *pratyutkrama* pattern 2_1). Therefore, 6 is the only number from which *karṣaṇa* is not permitted: the remaining numbers are all "extended" or "stretched" in some fashion (the sequence 1_{2345}, for example, shows 2 stretched from 1, 3 from 2, 4 from 3, and 5 from 4). Evidently the term *karṣaṇa* is considered inappropriate for extensions resulting from *pratyutkrama* or *atikrama*.

The expected duration of *karṣaṇa type* 1_2 is six *mātrās* (five *mātrās* if I follows). However, a T chanter allots eighteen *mātrās* to the sequence in the following rendition, where six general divisions are discernible.
Example 99 (T). 1 *mātrā*=eighth note. Gāyatram.

A NK performance of 1_2 for nearly thirty *mātrās*! But the six segments can be recognized here as well.
Example 100 (NK). 1 *mātrā*=sixteenth note. Sāmvargaḥ (GG 11.1).

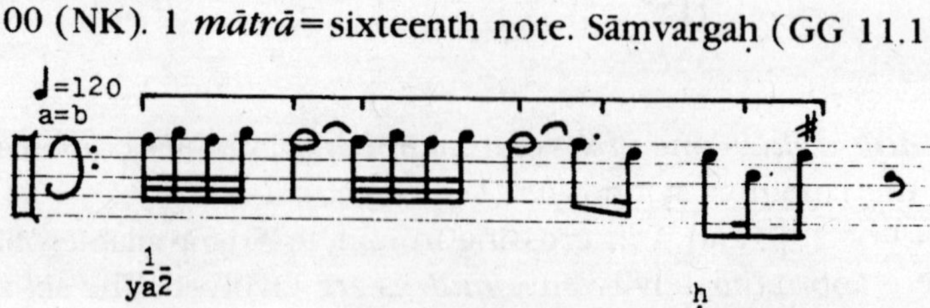

A special finger movement is associated with *preṅkha*: the thumb passes over the middle of the remaining fingers, from forefinger to little finger (see Howard

1977 : 80, 85).

Nine *mātrās* is the expected length of 1_{23} (eight *mātrās* if 2 follows). However, its execution by a T Sāmavedī shows that 1_{23} and 1_{2} are practically identical as far as performance is concerned.

Example 101 (T). 1 *mātrā*=eighth note. Vāmadevyam (ŪG 1.1.5).

There is melodic similarity in Karnataka as well, although in this performance 1_{23}, worth fourteen *mātrās*, has about half the value of the previously-described 1_{2}.It should be pointed out that other renditions of 1_{23} by the same chanter are more protracted.

Example 102 (NK). 1 *mātrā*=sixteenth note. Rathantaram (ĀrG 49.1).

The similarity of 1_{2} and 1_{23} undoubtedly stems from the fact that, in Jaiminīya manuscripts, the letter symbol *ṭ* occurs where 1_{2}, 1_{23}, and sometimes 1_{2} (which is also synonymous with *ṭ-ṭ*) appear in the Kauthuma notation (see Howard 1988). The Jaiminīya notation, which employed figure symbols at one time, predates that of the Kauthumas; it is a certainty that Jaiminīya is the original school of the Sāmaveda.

Theoretically, *karṣaṇa* of the type 1_{234} should possess twelve *mātrās*. In fact, a T realization of the sequence comes very close to this specification; but the division of each numeral into three parts is not possible.

Example 103 (T). 1 *mātrā*=eighth note. Rathantaram (ŪhyG 1.1.1).

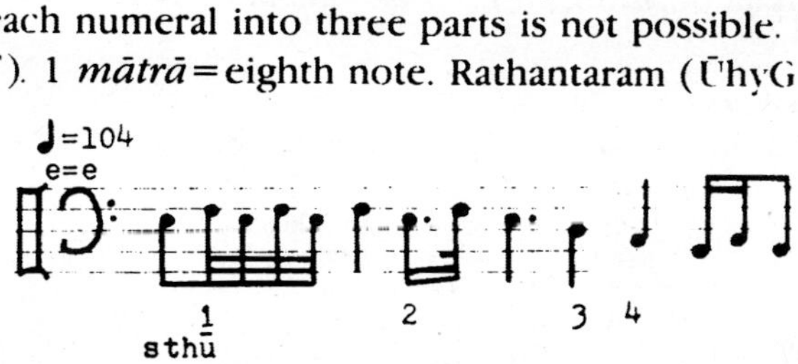

A Karnataka Brāhmaṇ extends the sequence to seventeen *mātrās* in the following performance. Here too segmentation into twelve sections is not feasible : if such division were attempted, numerals 2, 3 and 4 would be represented by only one segment each.

Example 104 (NK). 1 *mātrā*=sixteenth note. Gautamasya Caiva Parkaḥ (GG 1.3).

This 1_{234} type of *karṣaṇa* corresponds to the Jaiminīya sign *p* (see Howard 1988).

Fifteen *mātrās* should be assigned to 1_{2345}, fourteen *mātrās* if 4 follows. But nearly twice this duration is achieved in this T rendition. Speculation on a possible division into fifteen parts is fruitless.

Example 105 (T). 1 *mātrā* = sixteenth note. Hārivarṇam I (GG 383.1).

The NK singers likewise tend to double the time value. If one were to attempt some sort of partition, it appears that only one division would be associated with numbers 2, 3, 4, and 5.

Example 106 (NK). 1 *mātrā* = sixteenth note. Bṛhad Bhāradvājam (GG 3.1).

The sequence 5_6, worth six *mātrās*, is one of only two number combinations containing the *atisvārya* (6), the other being 5_{656} (see ML 1.19). The anticipated duration is approximated by a T chanter when 5_6 does not conclude the *parvan*; but when 5_6 is in final position, another Sāmavedī increases the duration to nine *mātrās*.

Example 107 (T). 1 *mātrā* = sixteenth note in the first example, an eighth note in the second. Janitram II (GG 484.2) and Rathantaram (ŪhyG 1.1.1).

A NK rendition of medial 5_6 has the characteristic nasalization and lasts precisely six *mātrās*.

Example 108 (NK). 1 *mātrā* = sixteenth note. Gautamasya Caiva Parkaḥ (GG 1.3).

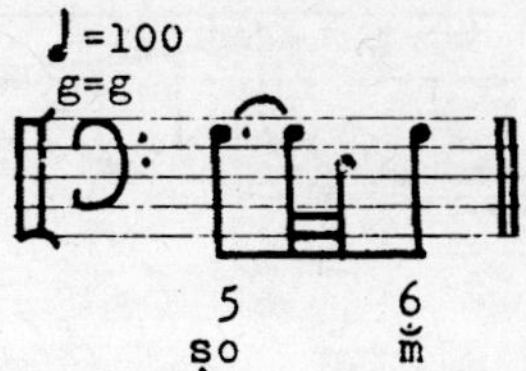

The sequence is one of several numbers and number combinations associated with the Jaiminīya symbol *pl* (see Howard 1988).

CHAPTER 2

1

This and the following rule properly belong in the first chapter, where the types of "syllables divorced from accentuation" are enumerated : Chapter 2 deals largely with exceptions to these rules. However, following the practice of the oldest Sāmavedic texts, this habit of overlapping the endings and/or beginnings of sections is clearly purposeful and reflects the desire, possibly manifested first in Jaiminīya texts, to avoid ominous interruptions (see Parpola 1981).

2

The three *svāra* varieties are very common coda configurations and are found most often on final syllables of chants. *Svāra* is to be distinguished from *svara,* which in Sāmavedic music denotes musical phrases and motifs. The three types of *svāra* are

2 1 111
harī3śrī2345ḥ (GG 195.1 : Āṅgirasāṃ Hariśrīnidhanam),
3 2111
rayā345im (GG 43.1 : Āyuḥ Sāma), and
3 111
ī2345 (ĀrG 54.1 : Mahāvairājam).

The third type is known universally as the *vairājanidhana,* but it is found in chants other than the Mahāvairājam. Those numbers of *svāra* with 1 placed above are worth one *mātrā* apiece (see ML 2.10). With the exception of the first 3 of 3_{2345}^{111}, which carries two *mātrā*s (see ML 2.3), the remaining numbers are worth three *mātrā*s. *Svāra* calls for a distinctive hand movement : the thumb passes over the tips of the remaining fingers, from forefinger to little finger (see Howard 1977 : 80, 86).

Svāra of the type 1_{2345}^{111} contains not nine but twenty *mātrā*s in this rendition by a T Kauthumin. However, nine divisions of the music are easily recognized. Example 109 (T). 1 *mātrā*=sixteenth note. Kaśyapasya Barhiṣīyam (GG 1.2).

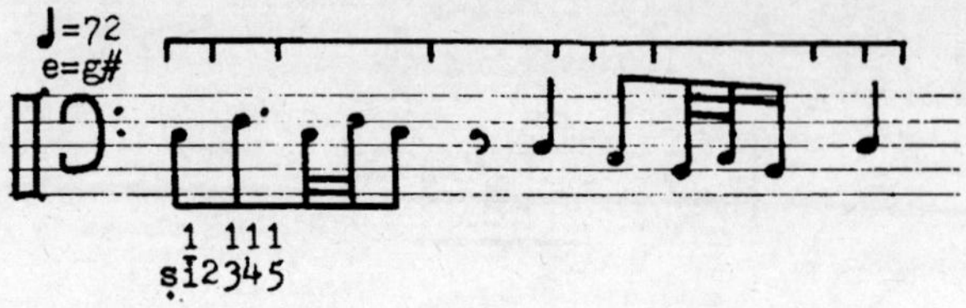

The NK Rāṇāyanīyas far exceed even this overextension: they give about fifty *mātrā*s to the sequence. Partition into nine sections would be highly speculative.
Example 110 (NK). 1 *mātrā* = sixteenth note. Mārgīyavam (GG 115.1).

The Jaiminīya counterpart of 1_{2345}^{111} is the compound symbol *ṭ-kh* (see Howard 1988.)

Svāra of the type 2_{345}^{111} consists not of six but of seventeen *mātrā*s according to the following T interpretation. Nevertheless, six general divisions are perceivable.
Example 111 (T). 1 *mātrā* = eighth note. Āmahīyavam (ŪG 1.1.1).

The NK singers too expand the sequence—to twenty-one *mātrā*s in this performance. Apportionment into six sections would be an exercise in conjecture.
Example 112 (NK). 1 *mātrā* = eighth note. Gāyatram.

Apparently 2_{345}^{111} was not a part of the original numeral notation, which utilized 3_{2345}^{111} in its place (see Howard 1988).

Svāra of the type 3_{2345}^{111} is composed of seveteen, as opposed to eight, *mātrās* in this T excerpt. An eightfold segmentation can be hypothesized.

Example 113 (T). 1 *mātrā*=sixteenth note. Vāco Vratam II (ĀrG *stobha,* before 94.1).

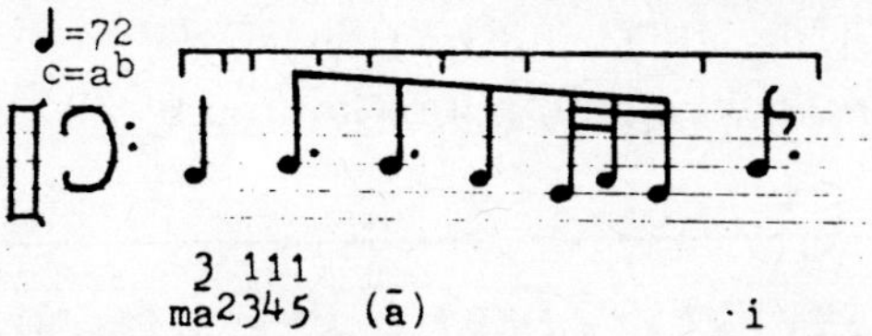

Typically, the NK Sāmavedīs lengthen even farther: they assign thirty-seven *mātrās* to the sequence in this extract. A theoretical division into eight parts can be put forth, however.

Example 114 (NK). 1 *mātrā*=sixteenth note. Sāṃvargaḥ (GG 11.1).

To 3_{2345}^{111} corresponds the Jaiminīya letter *kh* (see Parpola 1973: 19. 21; Howard 1988).

3

Under normal circumstances a "syllable divorced from accentuation" (*visvaram akṣaram*)—that is, a syllable with a time value in excess of that found on the accented *ārcika* syllables—contains three *mātrās* on each numeral. Theoretically, therefore, the sequence 1_{23} should contain three + three + three = nine *mātrās*. However, when *pratyutkrama* from 5 to 4, 3 to 2, or 2 to 1 takes place, the initial numeral in each case is worth two, as opposed to three, *mātrās*. Hence the sequence 5_4, is worth two + three = five *mātrās*; the numbers of 3_{234} are worth two + three + three + three = eleven *mātrās*; the sequence 2_1 bears two + three = five *mātrās*. In a case like $1_{23}2$, where the 3 is followed immediately by a 2-notated syllable, the sequence has this duration: three + three + two = eight *mātrās*. Similarly, under the circumstance $1_2 1$ *preṅkha* has three + two = five *mātrās*.

4

See ML 1.20, 22, 23 and 2.2 for illustrations of these combinations.

5

The sequence 2_1 in the cited example from the Aśvinoḥ Saṃyojanam is not an exception to the rule that "a syllable divorced from accentuation has triple measure on every *svara*." Neither is the *avanardana* of the Gāyatram (see Howard 1983 : 322-25; Howard 1986 : 342-46) an exception : 2_{1212} has the value three + three + three + three + three = fifteen *mātrās*. An interpretation of the *avanardana* by a T chanter shows that the five numbers of the sequence bear five + nine + five + ten + six = thirty-five *mātrās*. However, the stated apportionment into fifteen parts can be easily formulated.

Example 115 (T). 1 *mātrā* = eighth note. Gāyatram.

In a NK realization the *mātrās* are distributed five + eight + five + eight + two = twenty-eight. Guessing at fifteen divisions here will not be attempted.

Example 116 (NK). 1 *mātrā* = eighth note. Gāyatram.

6

In the excerpt

5r 3r 2
. . . pā / āvnā . . .

the syllable *pā* is divided between two *parvans* (see ML 1.24). Half the syllable is sung with the low *mudrā*, half with the third *mudrā*. The syllable is *not* sung as though notated

5 2
pā3vnā,

in which case the low *mudrā* would contain three *mātrās*, the third *mudrā* two *mātrās*: another school of Sāmaveda (the Jaiminīya) renders the text *sunota somapāvnāi* (they refer to the chant as Gautamam II). But in the Kauthuma-Rāṇāyanīya tradition each of the figures contains two *mātrās*, with the customary pause beween *parvans* inserted in the middle.

7

Since the low *mudrā* on the word *accha*, occurring in the passage

4 5 111
accha2 u/vā345 (GG 543.1: Vāsiṣṭham),

is found on a short vowel, it consists of one *mātrā*. The figure 2 contains the expected three *mātrās*. Therefore, the syllable *ccha* is worth a total of four *mātrās*.

8

Karṣaṇa of the $1r_2$ type, where the vowel in question bears the *r*-notation, is termed *dīrghakarṣaṇa* (see Simon 1913: 314, Howard 1977: 51-52). Each of the notated *mudrās* represents *svaras* that are long; hence each contains two *mātrās*. In the excerpt

1 r
praprā 2̂ (GG 35.1,4: Upahavaḥ I and Yajñāyajñīyam)

the second syllable has a duration of four *mātrās* (see Howard 1977: 51). Recordings of this type of *dīrghakarṣaṇa* are unavailable. The sequence has the compound symbol *ṭ-c* as its Jaiminīya parallel (see Howard 1988).

9

The $2r_3$ type of *karṣaṇa* is also attached to a vowel with the *r*-notation; this sequence likewise is termed *dīrghakarṣaṇa*. Each of the numbers is worth two *mātrās*; the last syllable of each of the above examples has a time value of four *mātrās*. Without consulting the oral traditions it is impossible to distinguish this type of *dīrghakarṣaṇa* from a form of the sequence *praṇata* (ss ML 3.5, Howard 1977: 70). The following NK example may be a legitimate instance of long *karṣaṇa*, although the *mātrā* values are far in excess of the anticipated four units: sixteen *mātrās* are associated with 2r, six with 3. Four sections of unequal length can be inferred from the music.

Example 117 (NK). 1 *mātrā* = sixteenth note. Pakthasya Saubharasya Sāma I (GG 110.1).

The Jaiminīya compound symbol *th-c* is the corresponding sign of the syllable notation (see Howard 1988).

10

The three types of *svāra* are 1_{2345}^{111}, 2_{345}^{111}, and 3_{2345}^{111} (see ML 2.1-2). Those figures with 1 placed above are, in theory, worth one *mātrā*. The superscribed 1 may be an outward indication of this unit value, or it may be used merely to differentiate *svāra* from the sequences 1_{2345}, 2_{345}, and 3_{2345}. In these cases the thumb touches, in turn, the finger corresponding to each number, whereas *svāra* calls for rubbing the thumb over the tips of the fingers. This peculiar hand movement renders it difficult if not impossible to ascertain the number of *mātrā*s connected with each numeral when the oral traditions are consulted.

11

From these examples it is obvious that *hrasvakarṣaṇa* can involve either 1_2 or 2_3 combinations (see Howard 1977:52), as is the case with *dīrghakarṣaṇa.* Recordings are unavailable.

12

The examples seem to indicate three ways in which a number notated above the text is approached from a number notated either above or within the text. In the first example, 1 is approached from 2, both figures notated above. The second example has 2 within the text, at the end of a *parvan*, rising to the superscribeed 1 at the beginning of the next *parvan*. The third example shows superscribed 2 approached, in the same *parvan*, by 3 notated within the text.

13

Once a number is notated, it holds true for all subsequent syllables, until a different number appears. Thus needless repetition of the numbers is avoided. Hence in the extract

1 r 2r
gṛṇāno ha (GG 1.1: Gautamasya Parkaḥ)

the figure 1 is valid for both syllables *gṛ* and *ṇa*. At the beginning of the *parvan*

2 1 2 1 r
draviṇsyur vipanyayā2 (GG 4.1: Śrautarṣam I)

numeral 2 is the notation for syllables *dra, vi,* and *ṇa.* In the excerpt

23r r2
vipāṃ jyotāi (GG 98.2: Prahitaḥ II)

syllables *pāṃ* and *jyo* bear the 3-notation. The section

4r r 4
ād it pratnā5sya retasāḥ (GG 20.1: Nidhanakāmam)

has 4 notated on *ād, it, prat,* and the beginning of *nā*. At the beginning of the *parvan*

5 r 4 5
agniṃ vo vṛdhāntām (GG 21.1: Saiṃdhukṣitam I)

figure 5 holds true for syllables *a, gniṃ, vo,* and *vṛ.*

Thus the ML demonstrates the validity of this rule of continuity by giving examples that utilize each of the five basic numerals (*mudrā*s). The *svara*s of the *kruṣṭa*- and *atisvārya-mudrā*s never occur on two successive syllables, a fact that underscores the relative unimportance of these *svara*s and suggests that they may in fact be later additions to the notation.

14

One-half *mātrā* is found

(1) on the *gati* vowel *i* of ognāi (GG 1.1: Gautamasya Parkah),
(2) on the *gati* vowel *u* of prestham vo hāu (GG 5.3 Auśanam),
(3) on the circumflexed 3 (*praṇata*: see ML 3.5) and the *visarga* of ṣu pravo23cā343h (GG 28.1: Somasāma),
(4) on the initial *svara* of *abhigīta* (see ML 3.7), represented by 7, and on the final *t* of nāy akramī2t (GG 30.1: Sauryam),
(5) on the *gati* vowel *i* and perhaps also on the hiatus (*vivṛtti*) between the syllables *vo* and *a* of vo agnāyā2i (GG 35.3: Śnausṭhīgavam),
(6) on the circumflexed 3, the numeral 4 of the sequence 45 (*utsvarita*: see ML 3.6), and the final *n* of tiyā3m cā5rā656n (GG 64.1: Ṛtusāma), (and)
(7) on the pause (*sthiramātrā*: sometimes notated *sthi*) after the exclamation *him* or *hum*, on the *gati* vowel *i* and the final *m*, and perhaps also on the hiatus between syllables *vo* and *a* of viśo viśo hum *sthi* vo6 ātithāim (GG 87.1: Viśoviśīyam Aidam Vā).

That ML 2.14 occurs in the second and not in the third chapter is another instance of textual overlapping; the material discussed above belongs with that of the next chapter, where fractional durations are examined. See the notes to ML 2.1.

CHAPTER 3

1

The two sounds are measured separately (see ML 1.15).

2

Most of the commentary on these sentences is "corrupt and hence not clearly understandable" (Sharma 1969: 17, n. 14). The commentator seems to imply that *gati* is worth one-half *mātrā* when attached to a long vowel, one *mātrā* when sung with an augmented vowel (but see ML 2.14, where the fractional duration follows an augmented vowel). Presumably, the preceding vowel would be worth one and one-half and two *mātrā*s respectively. But when *gati* is introduced by a semivowel it always lasts one *mātrā*, for *y* is treated as a consonant even though *gati* is not considered a separate syllable. The semivowel is inserted to prevent *vivṛtti* (hiatus) between two successive vowels. The oral traditions show scant adherence to these rules: in many cases *gati* bears a much smaller relationship to the preceding long or augmented vowel than the $1\frac{1}{2}:\frac{1}{2}$ and 2:1 ratios allow. See Examples 8, 24-25, 33, 50-53, 56, 63-64, 70.

3

Vinata, praṇata, utsvarita, and *abhigīta* are similar to the *svarita* accent due to the inherent complexity of rhythm and time counting: as will be seen shortly, the one-half *mātrā* interval is a characteristic of each. Moreover, the *svarita* is unlike the remaining accents (*udātta, anudātta, pracaya*), in that its innate musicality renders it difficult to distinguish long *svarita* syllables from those that are short (see Howard 1986:81-84, 89-91, 107-8). The same is true, for instance, in the case of *utsvarita*, which has a fixed duration regardless of vowel length (see ML 3.6). The *abhigīta* too has the long (two-*mātrā*) time value, although it appears almost exclusively on short vowels (see ML 3.7, Howard 1977:71-75). *Vinata, praṇata,* and so on are compared to the syllables of the *ārcika* for the reason that, like these syllables, they are always worth either one or two *mātrā*s. Thus they are distinguished from the *visvarāṇy akṣarāṇi*, which—not counting the exceptions—possess no fewer than five *mātrā*s (see ML 1.16, 2.3).

4

Vinata (see Simon 1908:522-23, Simon 1913:315, Howard 1977:69-70) starts with a *svara* of the thumb and ends with a *svara* of the forefinger. *Praṇata* (see Simon 1913: 315, Howard 1977:70) begins with a *svara* of the forefinger and concludes with a *svara* of the middle finger. *Utsvarita* (see Simon 1913:315-16, Howard 1977:70-71) begins with a *svara* of the ring finger and ends with a *svara* of the little finger. *Abhigīta* (see Burnell 1876 : xliv, Simon 1908:517, Simon 1913:316, Howard 1977:71-75) starts with a *svara* indicated by the forefinger and concludes with a *svara* of the thumb.

Originally *vinata* and *preṅkha* may have been one and the same (see Howard: 1977: 65, 113); with 2_3, 4_5, and 7 are associated the Jaiminīya symbols *t, pl,* and *y*, respectively (see Howard 1988). *Abhigīta* may have originally been identical to 2_1.

5

Vinata and *praṇata* are either long or short, despite the fact that they are occasionally attached to prolated/augmented vowels. In such cases the *r*-notation either should be present or should be understood to be present. Therefore, on prolated/augmnented or long vowels the *svara* of the higher figure is worth one and one-half *mātrā*; on short vowels it is worth one-half *mātrā*. The *svara* of the lower figure consists of one-half *mātrā*, regardless of whether the syllable is augmented, long, or short (see Simon 1913: 315, Sharma 1965: 40-41, Howard 1977: 69-70). The notation of *vinata* makes use of the *avagraha* or (in South India) the syllable *vi,* both written above the text; *praṇata* may or may not employ the circumflex above the numeral 3.

The second Gṛtsamadasya Madaḥ chant, on the verse *yaṃ vṛtreṣu,* has an example of *vinata* on a short vowel. The two Sammīlyam chants (ĀrG 51.4-5), on the text *pra yac cakram arāvṇe,* consist almost entirely of bisyllabic *parvans* concluding with *vinata* on short or long vowels. The Sammīlyam *sāmanṣ* are found also in the Ūhyagāna (ŪhyG 3.2.12-13: I am grateful to Prof. Tarlekar for informing me that the expression *sye* means, according to Sāmatantrasūtra 639, *rahasye*), but are set here to a different text. The Mahāvairājam (ĀrG 54.1), sung to the verse *pibā somam indra*, also contains examples of *vinata* on short and long vowels. Other *vinata* examples are from the Bharadvājinām Vratam (ĀrG 100.1), on the verse *abhī navante;* the second Vasiṣṭhavratam (ĀrG 114.2), on the verse *ud u brahmāṇi;* the Vārtraghnam (ĀrG 121.1), on the words *indrasya nu vīryāṇi;* the Kaśyapapuccham (ĀrG 147.1), on the verse *agnir asmi janmanā;* the Mahādivākīrtyam (ĀrG, sixth *stobha* after 155.1), on the words *dharma vidharma satyaṃ gāya;* the Tavaśyāvīyam (ĀrGP); and the Ānandaḥ (ĀrG 160.1), on the verse *ayaṃ gauḥ pṛśniḥ.* Examples of *praṇata* include

2r r 1
ā yāhī3 voi (GG 1.1: Gautamasya Parkaḥ),

2 r ˆ
tigmenâ (GG 22.1: Haraḥ I),

2 r
manye3 (GG 465.1: Bhāradvājam I), and

1r 2 r r
oṣadhīnā3m (ĀrG 157–159.1: Ādityavratam of the *śukriyaparvan).*

In the following example of *vinata* on a long vowel, a T chanter assigns not two but eight *mātrās* to the sequence. However, one can easily formulate a division into two equal sections: note that the final tone (one-half a section) would be connected with numeral 2.

Example 118 (T). 1 *mātrā*=sixteenth note. Rayiṣṭham (GG 512.2).

A NK singer adds even more *mātrās* than this; he gives fourteen units to *vinata* on a long vowel. Moreover, the music does not lend itself to the type of partition found in the previous example.

Example 119 (NK). 1 *mātrā*=sixteenth note. Lauśam I and II (GG 237.1-2).

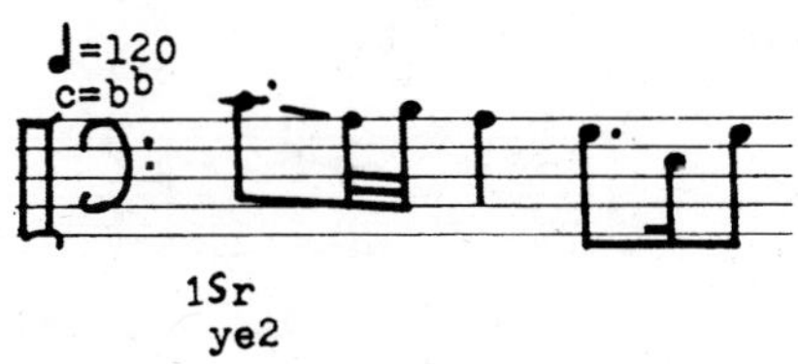

Praṇata too is seen to be much more elongated than the ML prescription states: seven rather than two *mātrās* are heard in this T performance of *praṇata* on a prolated vowel, where the distribution is four + three. Note that the two numerals of *praṇata* are effected on one and the same pitch. Thus the "bent" or "bowed" description of the sequence does not pertain to any musical feature but perhaps instead a salutatory role for *praṇata.* The time ratio $1\frac{1}{2}:\frac{1}{2}$ is not in

evidence here, but the first tone is discernibly longer than its repetition.
Example 120 (T). 1 *mātrā*=eighth note. Vāmadevyam (ŪG 1.1.5).

It is also the NK practice to exceed the prescribed duration and to realize the sequence on basically one tone. *Praṇata* on a prolated vowel is executed here. Nine *mātrās*, with the approximate distribution six + three, result.
Example 121 (NK). 1 *mātrā*=sixteenth note. Gautamasya Parkaḥ (GG 1.1).

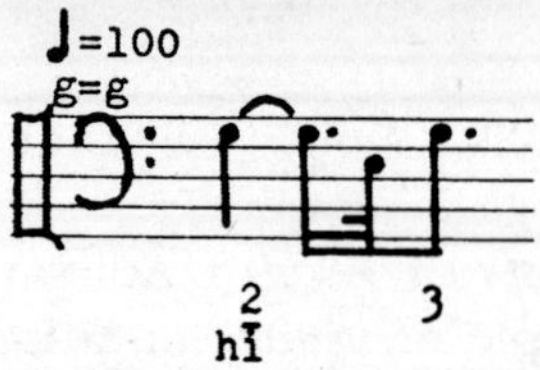

A syllable bearing *praṇata* is occasionally extended through the addition of one or more numerals. The sequence 2_{34} is such an example: in this performance, where it occurs on an augmented vowel, the *mātrās* are distributed four + four + two. Note that here 2 and 3 are of identical length, while 4 has one-half their value.
Example 122 (T). 1 *mātrā* = eighth note. Vāco Vratam I (ĀrG *stobha*, before 94.1).

Eighteen *mātrās* apportioned more or less equally among the three figures are achieved in this NK interpretation of 2_{34} on a prolated vowel.
Example 123 (NK). 1 *mātrā*=sixteenth note. Mārutam (GG 445.1).

6

A syllable bearing *utsvarita* has the numeral 4 above, followed by number 5 within, the line of text. The *svara* associated with the fourth *mudrā* lasts one-half *mātrā*, that accompanying the low *mudrā* one and one-half *mātrā*. *Utsvarita* ordinarily occurs on long vowels that have the *ārciko 'kṣarakālaḥ* (that is, the two-unit time value: $\frac{1}{2} + 1\frac{1}{2} = 2$). However, on rare occasions *utsvarita* is found attached to a short vowel (see Howard 1977: 61): only two examples of this exist in the entire Prakṛtigāna. In these two cases *utsvarita* retains the two-*mātrā* value and does not have the *ārciko 'kṣarakālaḥ* of one *mātrā*. *Utsvarita* is so named apparently because of a similarity between its execution and that of the *svarita* accent, when the latter occurs on a long vowel. Hence the term *utsvarita* is somewhat inappropriate to the two examples found on short vowels, although it is performed here in exactly the same way as on the long vowels. The falling quality attributed to the *svarita* by the *prātiśākhyas* (see Allen, 1953: 87-88) is found also as an element of *utsvarita* in that the *svara* connected with 4 is tonally higher than that associated with 5. In Sāmavedic chanting it is a general maxim that "the smaller (i.e., "higher") the numeral, the higher the *svara*," although exceptions are commonplace.

That *utsvarita* should last two *mātrās* is denied in this T rendition, which assigns eight + seven = fifteen *mātrās* to the sequence. The four descending pitches neatly divide the sequence into two segments. Apparently only the first tone is connected with numeral 4.

Example 124 (T). 1 *mātrā*=sixteenth note. Gautamasya Caiva Parkaḥ (GG 1.3).

Also exceeding the two-*mātrā* limit are these NK renditions, which contain six and seventeen *mātrās* respectively. The first specimen appears before a following 5, the second before 5_6. It is obvious that here the $\frac{1}{2} : 1\frac{1}{2}$ ratio between the two figures is completely ignored.

Example 125 (NK). 1 *mātrā*=sixteenth note. Gautamasya Caiva Parkaḥ (GG 1.3) and Raudram I (GG 115.2).

7

Abhigīta is indicated by the numeral 7 placed above the syllable in question. This number is a symbol of 2 followed by 1, for *abhigīta* is shown by first placing the thumb on the second finger, then flicking it upwards (see Howard 1977: 80, 85). Numeral 7 is found on both short and long vowels, but it has a fixed duration regardless: one-half *mātrā* is associated with figure 2 (representing the forefinger), one and one-half *mātrā* with 1, the thumb (the commentary, corrected above, reverses these values). An example of *abhigīta* on a short vowel is the following:

1r 7 4
stomāṃ rudrā23yā (GG 15.2: Jarābodhīyam II).

It is found on a long vowel in the excerpt

2 r 1 7r 111
janayant sūryam a3pāinvo arkā2345iḥ (GG 534.1: Vaiśvajyotiṣam I).

The chanting of *abhigīta* by a T Brāhmaṇ comes very close to the specified duration, surpassing it by only a single *mātrā*. Probably only the first pitch belongs to numeral 2.

Example 126 (T). 1 *mātrā*= sixteenth note. Sāṃvargaḥ (GG 11.1).

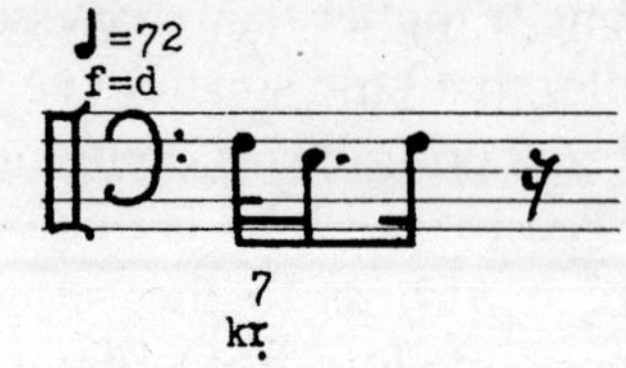

On the other hand, a NK Sāmavedī assigns six + eight = fourteen *mātrās* to the same syllable. Here the first two tones are undoubtedly associated with 2, the last two with 1.

Example 127 (NK). 1 *mātrā*= sixteenth note. Sāṃvargaḥ (GG 11.1).

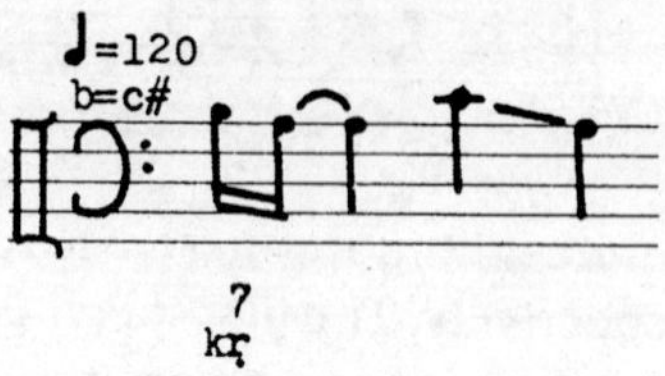

8

When *abhigīta* is extended through the addition of an extra number (always the figure 2), the result is *abhigītakṛṣṭa*. Only two instances of this occur in the entire Prakṛtigāna:

2 1 7 3 5
indraṃ vṛdhā / to2 dhvā234rāi (GG 151.1: Iṣṭāhotrīyam)
and
7 3 5
to2 kṣā234rān (GG 547.4: Āṣkāraṇidhanam Tvāṣṭrī Sāma).

The duration of the *svara* at the commencement of *abhigīta*—that is, that *svara* associated with numeral 2 (7 = 2 followed by 1)—is one-half *mātrā*, as is the case with ordinary *abhigīta*. However, the *svara* of the thumb is extended to two and one-half *mātrās* in *abhigītakṛṣṭa*. In order to avoid the confusion brought about by this fractional measurement of time, some teachers specify three *mātrās* for this *svara*. It can be assumed that the figure 2 notated immediately after 7 signifies a three-*mātrā svara* on the second *mudrā*. Hence a syllable bearing *abhigītakṛṣṭa* lasts either one-half + two and one-half + three = six *mātrās* or one-half + three + three = six and one-half *mātrās*

9

The letter *y* at the end of a word is worth one-quarter *mātrā*, as in the fragment

2r 1 4r r r 5
rāyāy ā23gne mahe tvā hāu (GG 93.2: Āsitam II).

This circumstance occurs when final *i* undergoes change to *y* when a different vowel follows. The one-quarter duration is encountered also as the value of initial *ṛ*, which is a composite of consonantal and vocalic elements (see Allen 1953: 61-62): the beginning or *ṛ* is discarded when the letter begins a word. However, the letter *r* bears the usual consonantal length, one-half *mātrā*. *Svarabhakti,* the vowel sound separating *r* from a following consonant (see Allen 1953: 73-75), usually a fricative, is worth one-half *mātrā*. But in the context *h* + *r* + sibilant, that *svarabhakti* followed by (or following) *r* lasts a full *mātrā*; one and one-quarter *mātrās* is the value of *r* and *svarabhakti* together.

10

In the Ṛgveda, "gandharva" usually refers only to a single individual, whose activities include measuring space and guarding Soma (see Macdonell 1898: 136). In the Mahābhārata there is

> . . . a distinction between divine gandharvas and human gandharvas . . . . . It says that "Gandharvas well versed in singing and skilled in dancing entertained the priests during the intervals between the ritual acts" (14, 88, 364 3C). . . . . .. That in the Veda gandharvas also mean real human beings, who were present at Vedic sacrifices, is clear from the Śatapatha Brāhmaṇa (11, 2, 3, 7): "Now when the ṛṣis were performing the sacrifice, the gandharvas came near to them. They looked on, thinking, 'Here, surely, they have done too much, here they have done too little.' And when their sacrifice was completed, they pointed it out to them . . . . . ." The gandharvas are spoken of in a hostile tone. . . . .(Parpola 1980: 23)

TRANSLATOR'S POSTSCRIPT

On being confronted with the numerous discrepancies between the edicts of the ML and the oral testimony of the two Kauthuma-Rāṇāyanīya traditions of Tamilnadu and Karnataka, one is tempted to conclude either (1) that the wrong traditions were selected for analysis, or (2) that all present-day Sāmavedic traditions are, from a historical perspective, corrupt. As a rejoinder to the first conclusion I should refer the skeptic to the transcriptions in Howard 1977 and to the analyses in Rajagopalan and Howard forthcoming, where, despite the limitation of materials, it is evident that not a single Sāmavedic community in all of India is in agreement with the ML on each and every point. In refutation of the second conclusion I should make the observation that the ancient Indian's concept of time was markedly different from that of our own. Now it is true that ML 1.14 declares explicitly that "in the *sāman* chants there is melody and evenness of tempo" (*vṛttisamaṃ ca gītaṃ sāmasu*). However, within a given tempo there seems to be a relativistic view of timekeeping:

> In Indian music of old times or present times, the time-unit of *mātrā* is to some extent relative. Hence counting the time-units by a metronome would not correctly help the understanding of the rhythm of *Sāman* chant (Tarlekar 1985: 15).

Even the eleventh-century commentator on the Nāṭyaśāstra, Abhinavagupta, expressed the belief that time is incapable of being measured absolutely. Both he and St. Augustine of Hippo (Algeria), who lived six centuries earlier, are of the opinion that "temporality in music is manifested by internal structure not by fixed durational values" (Rowell 1982: 27). With this philosophy of relativism in mind, is it any wonder that, for instance, an augmented syllable with ten times the duration of a short syllable is said to contain only three *mātrās?*

In the foregoing notes on the ML and its commentary only fragments of chants are transcribed for illustrative purposes. It will be instructive to include here a complete chant, the Gāyatram, in order to show the change in the value of *mātrā* from one syllable to the next—assuming, of course, that the larger segments and divisions postulated earlier correspond to *mātrās* and hence that the temporal unit's duration is not rigidly maintained as the length of a short vowel. The chanter is Śrī P. T. Govinda Aiyaṅgār of Srirangam, who sings in the Tanjore style.

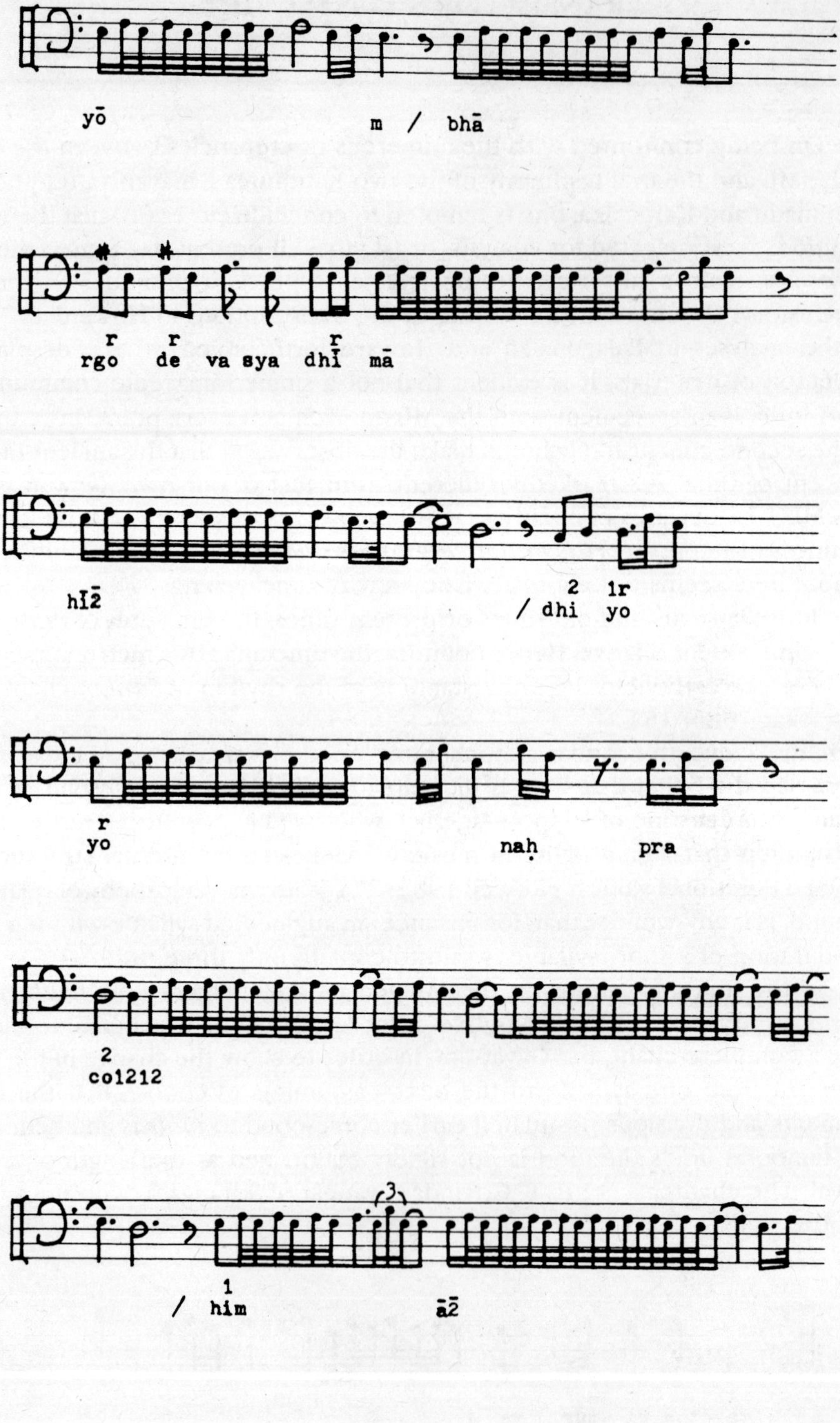
yō m / bhā
r r r
rgo de va sya dhī mā
2 1r
hī2 / dhi yo
r
yo naḥ pra
2
co1212
1
/ him ā2

In this performance a short syllable not followed by conjuncts or a change in notation lasts .29 second. The value of the *mātrā* stays the same or changes from syllable to syllable. In parentheses after each syllable is the number of *mātrās* that it should contain (according to my analyses above and not always according to the ML).

tat	($1\frac{1}{2}$):	. 29 + $\frac{1}{2}$ (.29)
sa	(1):	.29
vi	(1):	.29
tur	($1\frac{1}{2}$):	.29 + $\frac{1}{2}$(.29)
va	(1):	.29
re	(3):	.73 + .58 + .58
ṇi	(1):	.29
yōm	(1):	.73 + 1.16 + 1.02
bhār	(3):	.87 + .58 + .58
go	(2):	.29 + .29
de	(2):	.29 + .29
vas	($1\frac{1}{2}$):	.29 + $\frac{1}{2}$(.29)
ya	(1):	.29
dhi	(2):	.29 + .29
mā	(3):	1.02 + .44 + .58
hī	(6):	.87 + .87 + .87 + .87 + .87 + .87
dhī	(2):	.29 + .29
yo	(2):	.29 + .29
yo	(3):	1.02 + .58 + .73
naḥ	(2):	.29 + .29
pra	($1\frac{1}{2}$):	.29 + $\frac{1}{2}$(.29)
co	(15):	.48 + .48 + .48 + .87 + .73 + 1.02 + .48 + .48 + 48 + .1.02 + .73 + 1.16 + .58 + .58 + .58
him	(3):	.73 + .44 + .58
ā	(6):	1.31 + .73 + 1.02 + 1.02 + .73 + .73

dā	(2):	.73 + 1.02
yo	(3):	1.02 + .73 + .87
ā	(6):	.58 + .58 + .58 + 1.74 + 1.89 + 1.60

In this chant the *mātrā's* length varies from a low of .29 second to a high of 1.89 second. The concept of an adjustable or floating *mātrā* must be a trait of each and every Sāmavedic chant; otherwise many of the ML's statements would be utterly without validity.

BIBLIOGRAPHY

Allen, W. Sidney: 1953, *Phonetics in Acient India.* London: Oxford University Press.

Burnell, Arthur Coke, ed.: 1876, The *Ārsheyabrāhmaṇa (Being the Fourth Brāhmaṇa) of the Sāmaveda.* Mangalore: Basel Mission Press.

Dīkṣita, A.M. Rāmanātha, ed.: 1967, *Ūhagānam—Ūhyagānam.* Vedic Research Series, Banāras Hindu University, vol. 3. Varanasi: Banāras Hindu University Press.

Howard, Wayne: 1977, *Sāmavedic Chant.* New Haven and London: Yale Univerity Press.

— 1983: "The Music of Nambudiri Unexpressed Chant *(Aniruktagāna).*" *Agni: The Vedic Ritual of the Fire Altar.* Edited by F. Staal. Berkeley: Asian Humanities Press.

— 1986: *Veda Recitation in Vārāṇasī.* Delhi-Varanasi-Patna-Madras: Motilal Banarsidass.

— 1988: *The Decipherment of the Sāmavedic Notation of the Jaiminīyas. Studia Orientalia* (Journal of the Finnish Oriental Society).

Macdonell, Arthur Anthony: 1898, *Vedic Mythology.* Vol. 3/1a of *Grundriss der indo-arischen Philologie und Altertumskunde.* Strassburg; repr. ed. Delhi: Motilal Banarsidass, 1974.

Nārāyaṇasvāmī, R., ed.: 1958, *Grāmageyagāna—Āraṇyakagāna.* Pardi: Svādhyāyamaṇḍala.

Parpola, Asko: 1968–1969 *The Śrautasūtras of Lāṭyāyana and Drāhyāyaṇa and Their Commentaries: An English Translation and Study.* Vols. 42/2 and 43/2 of *Commentationes Humanarum Litterarum.* Helsinki: Societas Scientiarum Fennica.

— 1973, "The Literature and Study of the Jaiminīya Sāmaveda in Retrospect and Prospect." *Studia Orientalia* 43/6: 1–33.

— 1980, "The Epic Bard and the Early History of Indian Religions." Unpublished manuscript.

— 1981, "On thc Abnormal Khaṇḍa Divisions of the Jaminīya-Brāhmaṇa and the Jaiminīya-Upaniṣad-Brāhmaṇa." *Vaidika Saṃśodhana Maṇḍala Golden Jubilee Volume.* Poona: Vaidika Saṃśodhana Maṇḍala.

Rajagopalan, L.S., and Howard, Wayne: (forth-cóming) "A Report on the *prācīna* Kauthuma Sāmaveda of Palghat." *Journal of the Indian Musicological Society.*

Rowell, Lewis: 1977: "A Śikṣā for the Twiceborn." *Asian Músic* 9/1: 72-95.

— 1982, "7 Abhinavagupta, Augustine, Time and Music." *Journal of the Indian Musicological Society* 13/2: 18-36.

Sharma, Bellikoth Ramachandra, ed. : 1965, *Saṃhitopaniṣadbrāhmaṇam.* Tirupati : Kendriya Sanskrit Vidyapeetha.

— 1969, *Mātrālakṣaṇam.* Tirupati : Kendriya Sanskrit Vidyapeetha.

Simon, Richard : 1908 *Das Puṣpasūtra mit Einleitung und Übersetzung.* Vol. 23/3 of *Abhandlungen der philosophisch-philologischen Klasse der königlichen bayerischen Akademie der Wissenschaften.* Munich : n.p.

— 1913, "Die Notationen der vedischen Liederbücher." *Wiener Zeitschrift für die Kunde des Morgenlandes* 27 : 305-46.

Tarlekar, G.H. : 1985, *The Sāman Chants : A Review of Research.* Bombay and Baroda : Indian Musicological Society.

INDEX OF SĀMANS

GENERAL INDEX